Teacher Self

Teacher Self

The Practice of Humanistic Education

Jerome S. Allender

ROWMAN & LITTLEFIELD PUBLISHERS, INC.
Lanham • Boulder • New York • Oxford

ROWMAN & LITTLEFIELD PUBLISHERS, INC.

Published in the United States of America
by Rowman & Littlefield Publishers, Inc.
4720 Boston Way, Lanham, Maryland 20706
www.rowmanlittlefield.com

12 Hid's Copse Road, Cumnor Hill, Oxford OX2 9JJ, England

British Library Cataloging in Publication Information Available

Library of Congress Cataloging-in-Publication Data

Allender, Jerome S.
    Teacher self : the practice of humanistic education / Jerome S. Allender.
        p. cm.
    Includes bibliographical references and index.
    ISBN 0-7425-0994-X (alk. paper)—ISBN 0-7425-0995-8 (pbk. : alk. paper)
    1. Education, Humanistic.   I. Title.
LC1011.A55   2001
    370.11′2—dc21   00-066463

Printed in the United States of America

♾ ™ The paper used in this publication meets the minimum requirements of American
National Standard for Information Sciences—Permanence of Paper for Printed Library
Materials, ANSI/NISO Z39.48-1992.

Teachers are best
When students know them for their quiet presence,
Not so good when students obey and acclaim them,
Worse when they are despised.
But of good teachers, who talk little,
When the work is done and aims fulfilled,
It will be said, "We learned this together."

—Adapted from a poem by Lao-tse

"We speak in story form, as you know," the Dervish said, "and one
of the reasons for this is that you can listen to a story over and over
again, for each moment is different and will not repeat itself. Therefore the story will mean something different each time you study it."

—From *The Last Barrier* by Reshad Feild

Contents

Acknowledgments

DONNA ALLENDER

LEE SHULMAN * JUDY BASS * DEAN HOPMANN * VALERIE BERGMAN * DAVID VAN DUREN * KATHY MILLER * JENNIFER ROBINSEN * JOSEPH MCCALEB * EILEEN SEXTON * MARY ANN MANNINO * BETSY O'DONNELL * LINDA BELLINI * CAROLINE MELINE * CHA' KAULA * CHARLOTTE ZABACK * KATHY TELINGATOR * RACHELLE DORFMAN * CAROLE MITCHENER * FREDERICK LIGHTHALL * BARBARA MARKOWITZ * FELICIA ETH * JILL ROTHENBERG * GARY RASBERRY * VICKY PATTON * BETH FIFER * KATHY GARRETT * SHANNON MRKICH * ELIZABETH RAYER * MARY MANKE * JOCELYN WRIGHT * ANDREW HRYCYNA * FRANCIS CLARIDA * ED KIESS * ANN BARTHOLOMAY * MARY ELLEN BANEY * JOHN VON KNORRING * ALAN JONES * GLADYS TOPKIS

SHULMAN * LIS BIRKENKAMP * STEFAN VIDAL * RICHARD

There is a special group of people who, in their multiple roles as friend, professor, teacher, student, editor, literary agent, publisher, superintendent, and home schooler, gave of their time and hearts to thoughtfully criticize while supporting

ix

the writing in process. I imagine them as giving me, the teacher, an apple a day that nurtured this work over six years. The essential element in my view of teaching is relationship, and they all were willing to engage. They were open to being intrigued by the meanings I attributed to education and willing to respond with honest conversation.

Five of these people require an extra note. Donna Allender, my wife and a veteran classroom teacher, guided me in the initial years about the realities of elementary schools and high schools toward which my teacher education students were headed. Lee and Judy Shulman, longtime friends from our university days, took up a challenge, at year four, to advise me either to scuttle the book or to continue. Lee found concepts and theories missing that undergirded the stories that I was writing with my students. What Judy noticed encouraged prose more sensitive to the needs of readers and got me to realize that I needed Donna to coauthor a final chapter on Gestalt theory for teachers—taking over finally as the theoretician in our work together across forty years.

Former doctoral student and now colleague Lis Bass guided, with a respectful and ruthless hand and with a vision of the needs of readers, the writing of the final draft, page by page as the manuscript became shorter and shorter. Most recently, Dean Birkenkamp, my editor at Rowman and Littlefield, led the way for transforming the manuscript into a published book. I appreciated his enthusiasm and realistic advice.

Outside of people whose names appear in the apple, there are countless students through all the years I've taught, each of whom in some way has influenced me to be the teacher self I am writing about. Really, only a few are characters in these stories. I'm pleased that at least these few can be appreciated directly for their contribution to the book, especially the eleven student coauthors with whom it has been a joy to work. Thank you all for your help.

—Jerry Allender

Prologue

Each of us is quick to affirm that what is needed for teaching and preparing others to teach is intellectual, experiential, and personal knowledge; nevertheless, each of us has a preferred orientation. Traditionally, the order of importance has always been intellectual first and personal a distant third. For many in the field of education today, however, the rank order has reversed. I believe that learning to teach is primarily a task of self-development, a personal orientation. This premise is the starting point for weaving students' stories with my own so as to clarify the validity of self and better understand the value of personal knowledge for teaching. And these stories are the basis for the development of a Gestalt Theory for Teachers, which is presented in the last chapter.

There is still no shortage of people who feel that objective research—with reliable, valid, and generalizable results—provides the only really useful kind of knowledge, irrespective of the countless volumes of postmodern thinking that argue the contextual nature of truth. Over the years, it has been difficult to avoid the pressure that this view puts on the curriculum for educating teachers. What has been helpful is the expansion of other empirical research strategies that are conceptual and action oriented. Because these qualitative methods avoid numbers and emphasize description and conversation, the focus on interpretation as a valid way of knowing has flourished. These developments illustrate divergent ways of knowing.

Objectivity is an obsessive concern in Western culture, and this obsession distracts from a larger worldview.[1] Besides annoying encounters with narrow conceptions of objectivity in daily life, like academic committees paralyzed for lack of the right numbers, other experiences have been particularly troublesome for me as a teacher. My actions in the classroom, what I want education students to learn, and the research I do on the process of teaching have all been affected. More difficult yet, the overemphasis on objectivity masks the power of self-knowledge.

For the last six years, I have used the methods of narrative inquiry to study my teacher self.[2] When I began, Clandinin and Connelly had just proposed the use of narratives for exploring personal experience,[3] and Richardson had conceptual-

1

ized literary writing as a method of personal inquiry.[4] Stories written by students about their experiences in my classes were interwoven with stories of my reflections. I became aware of problems and imagined new possibilities. My teaching changed.

As a result, the students changed too. They became more articulate. The stories affected subsequent classes by giving support for the stronger expression of voice. With a flow of respect between teacher and students, and among students, supportive communities developed in which, though we certainly didn't all agree, there was an increased interest in listening to what others had to say. Empowerment and relationship grew hand in hand.

As my professional knowledge grew, I recognized that the exploration of self is intrinsic to educational research, whether or not we pay attention to its role. This is clear in Geertz's analysis, in another scholarly domain, of four grandparents of modern anthropology.[5] He shows how Lévi-Strauss, Evans-Prichard, Malinowski, and Benedict all write their own personalities into their respective ethnography. Or consider Wolf's *A Thrice-Told Tale*, in which one anthropologist writes the same events as field notes, an academic journal article, and fiction and raises the question about which is closest to the truth.[6] My students often chose the fictional version as the most true, revealing the power of personal writing as an unfamiliar source of data.

Methods of research are guided by root metaphors about the nature of reality, Sarbin says.[7] I chose to change old stories through the creative writing of new ones. The consequences of this restorying were profound. Restorying led to practical consequences in my classroom and to a change of standards by which the quality of teaching can be judged—by myself, my students, and others.

Writing narrative blurs the distinction between science and art. It is a personal view about quality teaching and learning that has given definition to the lens I use to study my teacher self. The stories are a mirror that encourages reflection on my teaching. But just as freedom in the classroom does not mean that students can do anything they want, or that any work of art is as good as another, research methods require a structure that sets standards of quality. Eisner's concept and discussion of connoisseurship, wherein he extrapolates from the methods of judging the quality of fine wine, and art in general, to the concerns of educational research, provide a good example.[8] Beyond knowing that knowledge is relative, we, or someone else, must create meaningful standards of quality from the resources of self.

What is unnerving is that standards once created do not remain constant. Our selves and our contexts change. When our response is to explore new methods, the standards can become foggy and distorted for a while. There are times we have to teach the way we were taught, as it were, hiding from what we don't know by living in an objective world. No less, the knowledge we hold dearly necessarily distracts us from other aspects of reality, and dysfunction is courted when the resistance to seeing multiple worldviews is too great. Pirsig proposes the concept of dynamic quality.[9] He argues that our prevailing static notions of quality are necessary for much of everyday existence. It is dynamic quality, though, balancing comfort with dissonance, that makes upsetting culture-shifting knowledge possible. This means that standards for judging quality sometimes have to be as fluid as the knowledge that is created.

Considering too lightly the workings of our inner worlds blinds us from the validity of self-knowledge. We have all been students for many years, and some of us teachers for many as well. Intellectual and experiential knowledge are important to the ongoing development of teaching skills, but preferring personal knowledge builds confidence in the power of self and self-study. When personal knowledge is in the forefront, conscious epistemological changes are feasible. Teachers can use this awareness in the classroom to better meet their own needs and those of the students. This text begins with the structure of a semester; moves through the stories, which are interrupted at the midpoint for a discussion of concepts that gird the stories; and concludes with an underlying Gestalt theory.

NOTES

1. Allender, J. S. 1991. *Imagery in teaching and learning: An autobiography of research in four world views*. New York: Praeger.

2. Sarbin, T. R. 1986. *Narrative psychology: The storied nature of human conduct*. New York: Praeger.

3. Clandinin, D. J., and F. M. Connelly. 1994. Personal experience methods. In *Handbook of qualitative research*, ed. N. K. Denzin and Y. S. Lincoln, pp. 413–27. Thousand Oaks, Calif.: Sage.

4. Richardson, L. 1994. Writing: A method of inquiry. In *Handbook of qualitative research*, ed. N. K. Denzin and Y. S. Lincoln, pp. 516–29. Thousand Oaks, Calif.: Sage.

5. Geertz, C. 1988. *Works and lives: The anthropologist as author*. Stanford: Stanford University Press.

6. Wolf, M. 1992. *Thrice-told tale: Feminism, postmodernism, and ethnographic responsibility*. Stanford: Stanford University Press.

7. See note 2.

8. Eisner, E. W. 1991. *The enlightened eye: Qualitative inquiry and the enhancement of educational practice*. New York: Macmillan.

9. Pirsig, R. M. 1991. *Lila: An inquiry into morals*. New York: Bantam Books.

1

Introductory Lecture

Directing a Semester's Learning

I think of teaching as if I were directing a play—an improvised play in which there are no lines for the players to read or only a few at most. There is, however, a specific structure that allows for and encourages all of the players, the teacher and the students, toward goals. Some of the time a teacher can act in a traditional manner. Other times, students can teach themselves in small groups. Most of the time, the teacher's predominant role is that of a director. The script is a set of notes, and at every juncture, detailed directions on how to proceed are given. What unfolds, in contrast, is undetermined and can be surprising. Paradoxically, the structure of the play has to be quite precise, while the hand of the director must be mostly invisible. This lecture describes the rhythm in a classroom over a semester.

To begin, teachers must build a climate of respectful relationships, between teacher and students and among students themselves. This is a key element that makes it possible to have a sense of control while creating conditions that allow for addressing a wide range of student differences. The teacher's role is to encourage thinking and self-expression. For a director, the belief in students' ability to guide their own learning should be stronger than an emphasis on right answers.

In this learning environment, students might mistakenly believe that there is no pressure to do assigned work. As with any style of teaching, though, a clear structure is essential. Without regular preparation, improvisations are flat or, worse, simply opinionated. For the dialogue to be energetic, focused, and constructive, students have to conscientiously do their class assignments. Then, students will speak their lines in the play with strength and understanding.

Along with pressure to do their work, students should feel a teacher's caring and trust. This does not mean that students are peers. Someplace between friendship and constrictive authority is a classroom leader who facilitates the development of commitment and community. Students feel special when they understand that the value of a teacher's ideas is not so dominant that the value of

5

theirs is lost. What teachers say and do is important, but it is also true that people learn best when they are given choices and encouraged to express their own views.

Together, teachers and their students need to be engaged in joint learning ventures. This attention to interpersonal interaction and desire for mutual coop-eration reflects a core tenet of humanistic education. In this philosophy, the pri-ority of person is higher than curricular goals. Both are necessary, but students' needs come first. One challenge is finding ways to successfully respond to each student's individual needs.

Because a typical class has twenty-five students or more and only one teacher, this is a tall order. There is no question that giving attention to one student can conflict with the needs of others. Furthermore, the major concern, rather than to meet the needs of students, can often be the problem of maintaining control. For some teachers, the concern is sufficiently ubiquitous that they are guided mainly by fears that students will cross the boundaries that they want to set. But when students feel they are special, there are fewer behavior problems.

Instead of worrying about control, I focus on conversation. Within the struc-ture of the play, classroom interactions, from the outset, can demonstrate the social rules of the learning environment—better than the words in a handout or what might be posted on a blackboard. These conversations establish what is expected of students and what they can expect of the teacher.

When students first enter a classroom, the teacher can bank on them wanting to know about expectations because students want to succeed. Even a student who has the habit of doing as little as possible will be interested in what will happen. Students are curious about the personality of the teacher, the rules of attendance, what has to be read, what written, the work that will be assigned in and out of class. Tapping students' curiosity about their own welfare is an easy place to start. But for a teacher to suggest that the curriculum could be changed as a result of an opening conversation would be misleading. Just as social interac-tions require boundaries for mutually respectful relationships, they are also needed so as not to lose sight of the curriculum. However, a conversation that invites interpretation and additions, and shows room for choices, demonstrates the realness of a joint venture.

The mechanics of designing classroom activities so that discussions like these flow smoothly, and do not get seriously off target, are unfamiliar. They depend on a teacher's attentive listening as well as creative instructions that clarify the limits within which the discussion will feel relevant—to the teacher and to the students. The listening works if there is a high level of acceptance of a student's thoughts and a commitment to reframing what is unacceptable in terms that bring the teacher's and student's thinking closer together. As the teacher models listening, students will feel special because of the careful attention to what they are saying.

The instructions that guide an activity must include questions for which a wide range of responses make sense and contribute to the discussion. These I call true questions. Not every student necessarily will want to answer them, but anyone could because the answers reflect personal thinking and opinion. In this way, students learn that what they have to say counts. Once a student has had a turn or two, the teacher must also insist that he or she listen to others.

Relevance is maintained most easily when the social and academic boundaries of classroom activities are broad enough to be rarely breached. In the event that this happens, it is an opportunity for the teacher to gently exercise authority. The students' experience of being carefully heard builds a receptivity to the exercise of authority. It is a kind of slack that allows any relationship to function with less difficulty. A sense of psychological safety is also increased from knowing that the teacher is in charge when conflicts arise.

Students, too, can be directed to ask questions of each other. They do not come to a teacher as blank slates but, rather, with varieties of prior knowledge. Honoring this knowledge establishes that learning is not solely dependent on the teacher. It helps to clarify that the role of the teacher is as someone who sets the stage for learning, rather than the one who is the only source of learning. Asking students to talk with each other about what they know enables them to share information, experience the value of listening to others, and realize that they also guide their own learning.

Once students are comfortable with the way the class functions, the focus on the curriculum can be heightened. The first concern is to make sure that students are finding personal value in their work. There is always a need to evaluate whether assignments have been done correctly, but more important is helping students to see that their efforts are meaningful. Compelling texts, choices, open-ended questions, and assigning homework that is an integral part of classwork involve students in their learning. Directing students to notice where their work is strongest helps them to identify aspects of the curriculum with which they can feel connected. What students learn must be about themselves as much as it is about the larger world of knowledge they are attempting to master.

Tasks that relate to students' everyday experiences reveal connections between individual needs and the goals of a lesson. Such tasks create a common language for discussion between the teacher and the students and among the students themselves. These experiential assignments make it possible for students to relate the curriculum to their lives. The assignments need to be tilted so that success is likely, but regardless, talking about these experiences is usually not difficult for students. Because they are about work that has been assigned, discussion will satisfy the teacher's goals equally well.

The natural interest that people have for talking about their own experiences makes it comfortable for students to share their learning. The discussion can be facilitated by the teacher in a traditional manner. When one thinks about teaching as a play, though, there are endless numbers of small group activities that can be invented to structure a discussion that is both entertaining and instructive. The advantage of group work is that the teacher, released from traditional responsibilities, can attend fully to the role of a director. While moving from group to group, there is time to listen, make brief comments, and redirect the focus of the discussion when it loses sight of larger learning goals. There are times when asking students to work in small groups causes tensions in a class, so it is also the director's job to modify instructions occasionally to minimize interpersonal conflicts. After a while, most students notice that working together is fun and productive.

Inventing a highly motivating activity that keeps students on task tempts one to use it over and over again. In my opinion, a successful activity should not be repeated within a semester with the same group of students. The probability is that it will soon lose its power to focus students' attention. A rule of thumb (which I admit to breaking occasionally) is to introduce new and different activities every week. With experience, the flow of activities can be sequenced to build a dramatic effect, as in a play, over the course of a semester.

Building drama, however, does not mean steadily upping the challenge. When the curriculum is in the center of students' attention, there is room to introduce a learning climate that feels easier for a while. This allows for finding increased fit between the curriculum and individual learning styles. With less pressure, students are free to explore ways of contributing to class that suit them best. They also reveal to the teacher their uniqueness so that future lessons can be targeted toward each student's potential.

For me, the use of visual communication and mental imagery with which it is strongly connected is an avenue to this ease. Visual tasks are fun. They are a welcome change from familiar classroom communication that revolves around spoken and written words. Though unfamiliar in classrooms, imagery, present in every human mind, can be adapted to activities that have special personal involvement. Also, imagery shows connections with other ways of communicating that are not centered on linguistic and logical modes of thinking.

We need only follow the example of teachers of young children who readily introduce drawing, music, and kinesthetic activities into their classes. It's a mistake, though, to think that there are not learners in every class of students, however old, who need opportunities to learn in other than traditional ways. The variety itself is attractive to students. The least difficult place to begin is with drawings of diagrams and pictures. What is striking about adding them into the ongoing conversation is how many more students participate. There is a shift in classroom interaction that comes from the playfulness of drawing itself and the ways in which pictures and diagrams allow students to see lessons from a different perspective. Even quiet students are sometimes eager to speak about what they draw.

When using imagery, the classroom climate becomes more relaxed. It is similar to what happens when students play games as part of their classwork. They are attracted to games as if by some gravitational pull. Likewise, with activities that stimulate visual and other nontraditional thinking, there is a compelling ease that surrounds them. This relaxed interchange of ideas enhances the ability to improvise. Playfulness and the idea of teaching as a play intertwine.

Students are receptive now to both intellectual and emotional challenges. The history of mutually respectful conversations has led to the development of relationships with the teacher and with each other that make it reasonable to expect a greater willingness to risk. Activities can be introduced that temporarily restrict the normal broad parameters within which the class operates. These activities restrict the freedom to participate or not—to choose what a student wants or doesn't want to do. Tasks insist that students suspend their worries about making mistakes and try to do what they imagine they can't do. As in role-playing, a person tries on ways of thinking and acting that are not in one's repertoire.

When a teacher pushes harder, though, heightening the risks that are involved, students can become unsure of whether their needs for safety are being met. For example, when role-playing is introduced as a learning activity, a student might feel pressed to play a role that turns out to be highly uncomfortable. Partly, the expansion of the slack that has been growing in class helps to compensate for discomforts that are engendered, but the teacher also risks that some students will be upset.

One avenue for soothing feelings is to sensitively adjust the difficulty of an activity while it is in progress—for the class as a whole, for a particular group, or for an individual. Some students feel that this is manipulative and/or unfair, but these adjustments are a legitimate responsibility of the teacher. When pressed, I have said to students, on occasion, "You don't have to *want* to do this task, but you have to do it." I once told a competent, articulate, likable student—whose participation regularly crowded out others in class—that he was not permitted to speak during the first half of a discussion that was meant to draw in several quiet students. My demand at that moment was an affront to him and a few other members of the class. But after the discussion, they were better able to understand why I made the decision.

Still, difficult learning carries the potential danger of painful embarrassment. No kind of teaching is immune to causing pain that interrupts the learning process. I think this is because learning in many ways is essentially a reimaging of self, and all of us have to contend with a strong desire not to change. The function of these activities is to help students discover whether long-standing images of themselves are interfering with learning new skills. One relatively safe strategy is to make the making of mistakes normal. Teachers have to communicate to students that it is possible to make mistakes, and laugh at oneself, without penalty or loss of respect. In this context, mistakes are productive and insightful. Not all learning is easy, and some learning means moving outside of a comfortable space.

Another strategy is to change how small groups function. At the outset, it works to form new groups every time a new activity is initiated. Students get to know many of their classmates better. As a result, they develop preferences for whom they would like to work with closely. With this information, as a part of heightening challenge, it is practical to form long-range groups in which students can develop stronger ties with each other. These ties serve to increase the amount of support individuals will receive from fellow students. The teacher can have higher expectations and count on students to develop a commitment to working together over a period of time.

The greater commitment to working together enables students to take turns teaching other group members. The idea that the best way to learn something is by having to teach it has ready application in this situation. The distance between the level of knowledge of the "teacher" and that of the other students is reduced because they are peers, yet the challenge motivates everyone in the group. There is less stress and more learning for more students because independent thinking and self-expression have already been encouraged. Responsibility for teaching substantial parts of a lesson plan is feasible. The sense of productive independence is sometimes exhilarating.

At the same time, the teacher's role as a director is further widened because of increased opportunities to interact with students and groups individually. For a director, there is time to assist students in their preparations for teaching. Students can also be observed more closely, and a teacher can reflect on his or her actions as a facilitator—even as the play progresses.

The willingness to accept challenge starts with emotional strength and ends up stretching the intellect. It is necessary to balance these aspects of learning. Traditional approaches to education give us little practical knowledge about how to achieve this balance. When I assume, however, that important learning of any kind requires mental restructuring, then I can see that resistance is normal. The habit has been for teachers to view resistance negatively and simply push harder on students irrespective of how often this approach leads to failure. If learning involves a restructuring of self, the teaching activities need to be designed to support the process. The teacher's work is to reframe resistance so that students' negative behaviors become useful to the lesson.

As the end of a course of study nears, attention turns to evaluation. This is an opportunity to consolidate learning. Evaluation is important for both teachers and students, but in viewing it only as a means of judging students' progress, one runs the danger of missing students' needs to capture and reflect on what they have learned in a larger context. Learning that is not attached to such a context is less likely to translate into stable, practical knowledge. What works for my classes is to use the evaluation process for pushing students harder while helping them see their learning in a multitude of connections. In raising the level of challenge to its high point, the classroom play is brought to a dramatic climax. This feeling of drama reinforces the restructuring of self.

This is when many students are given full responsibility as teachers, not only of their groups but of the entire class. Of course, the teacher/director must continue to design activities with boundaries. As always, some must be in place. But here, the teacher only works closely with students to be sure that they are thoroughly prepared. Acting as teachers, students are then given more responsibility and freedom than ever before. This is an exciting time because the outcomes are largely unexpected. Yet two things are sure to happen: When students are teaching, they maximize the power of their knowledge because they are in charge, and the other students sense their own authority because the teacher is a peer.

Finally, I ask students to draw what they have learned over the course of the semester. In my case, this is a task that consolidates what has been learned about the art and science of teaching. This is the denouement, and the activity works wonders. Every student becomes articulate in front of the whole class. Students standing in front of their drawings talk freely about what they have learned about teaching and themselves as teachers—and this knowledge is always important.

What follows are experiences of a teacher and his students that illustrate and explore this approach to teaching. For the final paper of an undergraduate education course, called the "Art and Science of Teaching," the students were asked to write short stories that revealed their learning during the semester. I chose some of these papers as a basis for writing my stories. After these were combined, each student author read and approved the final version. We were able to agree that the interwoven stories you will read are fair accounts of what actually happened.

2

First Week

Cast/Roll (in order of participation)

Jerry Allender:	Author, director, teacher
Crystal Hicks:	Author, narrator, student
Steve M.:	Discussant
Kim:	Discussant
Joann:	Discussant
Tracy:	Crystal's partner
Leslie:	Raises hand
Mike:	Raises hand
Steve T.:	Notices sleight of hand

The scene is a college classroom in the fall of 1993 on the seventh floor of Temple University's Education Building. It's a Monday afternoon. The second scene is the same, on a Wednesday afternoon, two days later. The course is the "Art and Science of Teaching." The students, twenty-nine in all, are sitting in chairs without writing arms in one large circle. Not quite half of the students are white women of typical ages for undergraduates. The other students are a mix of African American, Asian, Latino, and some older returning students of various ethnicities. They all have families in or close to Philadelphia. Their commitment to becoming teachers, even with their doubts, is very sincere. The scene opens with the teacher, sitting in the circle, bringing the introductory lecture to a close.

∼

I love the story that Lily Tomlin tells as the bag lady, Trudy, in the play *The Search for Signs of Intelligent Life in the Universe.* She has been hosting two aliens from another planet and teaching them about the ways of people on Earth. They are learning a whole lot rather easily, but they are having great difficulty understanding the meaning of goose bumps. One evening at the theater, the three of them are watching one of those wonderful plays where you find yourself crying and laughing at the same time. In the dark, they turn to Trudy and whisper that they finally figured out goose bumps. It is moments like these that move us all, moments when a true understanding is reached with others. The lights go up, and Trudy curiously asks the two aliens why they liked the play so much. "The play?! The play?! We didn't know we were supposed to watch the play." Trudy had forgotten to tell them to watch the play. They had been watching the audience. Watching a group of strangers, sitting together in a darkened theater, crying and laughing at the same time, that's what gave them goose bumps.

This story captures what happens when I am helping you learn to become teachers. The play, the performance, and the audience could represent three essential elements in a classroom. The script is a body of knowledge, the performance is how I teach, and the audience is you, my students.

However, the minute I start exploring this metaphor carefully, there are complications. It is too simple to say that the assigned books contain all the knowledge I want you to learn. You bring a wide range of experiences from your years as students in classrooms. More than this, you have had a variety of opportunities to teach already. Many of you have taught in Sunday school and worked in summer camps. Also, *how* I teach is no small matter in what I communicate to you about the art of teaching.

Furthermore, while the aliens weren't watching the play, it still had to be good enough to get the reaction it got from the audience. Without the reaction, there would have been little of interest for the aliens to watch and no chance for goose bumps. The fact that they are watching the audience, not the play, raises an intriguing question about the main focus in the classroom. I don't believe it's the books, but like the play they do have to have an impact on you.

Finding books like these has not been easy. To begin with, there is pressure to choose from among the many standard texts that are published every year. Generally speaking, they are really quite dull. At least, this has been the reaction that my past students and I share. There is also pressure to cover the most accepted academic concepts. . . . (fade)

(It's moments like these that I wish I could actually fade in real life. So sure of the importance of what I have to say, my teacher self gets a little out of hand. Soon I will recognize the dangers of boring the students and stop lecturing. Meanwhile, it's a good place to look at this class from a student's viewpoint.)

Let me introduce myself. I'm Crystal Hicks. I'm an undergraduate art education student. It's Monday afternoon, and I've been listening to Professor Allender's opening lecture for his course on the art and science of teaching. So far, it is interesting and a bit strange. I like how he listened carefully before he answered a few questions that students asked in the beginning. On the other hand, he is overenthusiastic and not clear yet about what we have to do in this course. Plus, there was one outrageous remark. He said that, by the end of the week, with little effort, some of us would know all of our classmate's names, all twenty-nine. I don't think so.

Me? I'm usually shy. I pay close attention. I'm a good student. My motivation

in this course is high because I know I want to be a teacher. But I won't participate much in discussions.

Right now, we're sitting in a large circle going over the first page of the syllabus. There are seven books, and each of us has to choose four. Instead of telling
about them directly, he is asking us to imagine what they are about from the
titles and the authors' names. It's a curious way to introduce the course, but at
least it isn't boring.

The adventurous ones are raising their hands. When he calls on you, you have
to tell your name and then say anything you want. Steve is offering an opinion
about *Growing Minds* by Herbert Kohl. He imagines it is about children's development and how teaching methods need to be sensitive to different stages of
learning. Professor Allender says this is a reasonable guess, because the title leads
people to think so, but is not actually what the book is about. He tells Steve that
it is much more a series of classroom vignettes, mostly successful, by a long-time
experienced teacher.

Kim offers an opinion about *Teaching for the Two-Sided Mind* by Linda Williams. She thinks it is about the ways that our minds function in two distinct
ways, one linearly and the other holistically. Her guess was on target. Good for
her.

I am curious to know about *Totto-chan* by Tetsuko Kuroyanagi. I'm not about
to talk in class, but I don't have to. Joann is suggesting that it is a book about
the Japanese educational system. The answer she gets is yes and no. The book is
about a school in Japan. However, it is one that existed during the 1930s. The
author is a popular Japanese television personality, and she has written about her
childhood school. It's sad to believe, but she was expelled from public school for
not paying attention when she was in first grade.

The school she got into was very unique. Students were given a lot of individual choice, and class lessons were taught in unusual ways. Music and art were
particularly important, and there often were field trips. Professor Allender says
that Kuroyanagi tells wonderful stories that touched him deeply. He has assigned
the book because it shows how much an educational environment can differ
from our normal expectations. I think this one will be my first choice. . . . (fade)

(I'm pleased with how the discussion is going. Without getting too long-
winded, the students are introducing themselves to me and each other. The likelihood of confusing tangents is low. The focus on the books is where I want it,
and the emphasis on their imaginations seems to be keeping their interest and
curiosity high.)

(Crystal) I'm back. We've finished discussing the books we will be reading,
and we have been asked to introduce ourselves to one person sitting next to us
in the circle. I like this. I get to meet and talk with someone without having to
embarrass myself in front of the whole class.

Tracy is my partner. She seems nice. We're supposed to look over the list of
expectations for the course and come up with questions about anything we don't

understand. Most of them are fairly clear. Attend class. Read four books. Two papers. Here is an unusual one. He wants us to telephone him if we are going to be absent. He also wants a journal of what happens in class. It's supposed to provide material for discussion and writing our papers. I wonder if it is has to be different than my regular notes.

Tracy and I just found an expectation that is new to the both of us—four experience experiments. They will be assigned over the course of the semester, and the first one is due next week. Tracy is raising her hand to get Professor Allender to clarify the assignment.

Interesting. We have to plan and teach a half-hour lesson to one of the students in our field placement. This is a little scary. I knew we would be helping a teacher in a local school for two hours a week, but it didn't dawn on me that we would start teaching so soon. This is my first education course. Well, one good thing I can say is that the course won't be all theory.

The assignment makes sense to Tracy and me. We have to read two chapters from any of the seven books and apply one or two ideas from our reading that we think might improve our skill as a teacher. We can teach the child any subject we want, and all we have to do is write up what happens in a one-page paper.

I must admit that this way of discussing the syllabus is better than what happened in another course earlier today. I'm more awake, and the period is passing quickly. In fact, there's not much time left. I better pay attention. Professor Allender is introducing the course themes. . . . (fade)

Turn now to the third page of the syllabus. These are the four themes we will be covering in the next fourteen weeks: creating an effective learning environment, the cognitive side of learning, the emotional side of learning, and the development of teacher self. Notice that there are about a half dozen questions listed under each theme. These are the guiding questions we will address over the course of the semester. We don't have time today to review all of them in class. Instead, join up with your partner again and choose the one theme that first draws your attention. Look, together, over the questions I've written for this theme and think about what other questions you would like us to be asking. Class will end with each group sharing the theme that was chosen and one or two of the questions that you added. . . . (fade)

(I have to limit the group discussions to five minutes in order to leave ten minutes to hear their suggestions. We could use more, but it's enough. Some of their ideas will be heard, and a few more people will get introduced. This class already seems promising. Following my unusual instructions hasn't inhibited the discussion, and that's a good sign.)

(A few minutes later) I really appreciate your input. These are great questions. There are a few that never occurred to me, and I'm pleased to add them. I can see that this semester is going to be a challenging learning experience—for me as well. Recognize, too, that planning this course has already become a joint venture. Enjoy the rest of your afternoon, and I'll see you on Wednesday.

Please form the chairs into a large circle again today. I'm passing out a paper written by a student from last semester. It was her first experience experiment. It will help you see what I mean by next week's assignment.

This experience experiment was based on a concept from *Totto-chan*. Totto-chan is a name. It is what Kuroyanagi was called when she was a little girl. The concept the student chose comes from the book's first chapter. The day that Totto-chan arrived at the new school, the headmaster took her into his office and invited her to talk about anything she liked. When she would come to the end of what she was saying, the headmaster asked her if there was anything else she wanted to mention. According to the tale, they were engaged in conversation throughout the morning until lunch. Maybe the time is exaggerated, but, even so, there is something very powerful in the way the headmaster listened to Totto-chan. This experience experiment builds on this idea of listening.

Take a few minutes to read this paper and then write a discussion question on an index card.

(The class is quiet for a few minutes. Moments like these are unusual, but I understand why teachers like them. I have time to think. I've only done this activity once before. It replaces one in which students wrote a personal question about what they wanted to learn during the semester. The discussion that those questions generated was too open-ended for the first week of class. My new strategy has been doubly useful. It gives direction for the first experience experiment, and it stimulates a discussion that can be more easily kept to the task.)

Okay, hand in the cards and be sure your name is on them. I'm going to shuffle the questions and pass them back. We'll trade if you get your own. What you have written is from the point of view of your teacher self. This concept will come up regularly, and it is the main focus of the fourth theme.

For now, whenever your question fits in the discussion, call on the person who wrote it. Be the teacher in class. Ask the person to answer the question, listen carefully to what he or she says, and then make some thoughtful comment in response. That's all. You've heard of king or queen for a day? This is teacher for two minutes.

When you are called on, become aware of your student self. That won't be hard because it is your normal role in class. Because you wrote the question, though, notice that there is a momentary awareness of both your teacher self and your student self at the same time. I find that this is unusually helpful for learning how to become an effective teacher. And meanwhile, the discussion will continue to introduce ourselves to each other. Somebody start. . . . (fade)

It's me, Crystal. This man is a sneak. The way he set up the discussion, everybody is going to have to participate before class is over. I feel like I've been trapped, but it's not too disastrous. At first I thought I might get away with not having to call on the person whose question I have. Twice, a general discussion started when several other people added their comments, and I was sure we would run out of time before getting around to every one. No such luck. Professor Allender listened patiently, and then, quietly interrupting, he asked for the next teacher. Oh well, I'm sure I can manage two minutes without bruising my ego. I guess I'll get it over with. . . . (fade)

Well, that wasn't so bad. I don't think my comment was too coherent, but then, no one seemed to notice. Actually, the discussion we're having is quite interesting. What's amazing is that if some new person walked in right now, it would be unclear who the teacher is. Professor Allender's gray hair might give him away. Still, there are a couple of older students who could easily draw attention—especially if one of them was in the middle of calling on a student. It's nice not to have the regular talkative types hogging up all the air space. This kind of discussion is fairer. If this keeps up, I might learn to participate.

It looks like we might be ending early. There are only a couple of people left who haven't had their turns. This class is enjoyable, but I wouldn't mind a little extra time.

Oops! Now that the we're finished with the discussion, would you believe that he has just asked us to put down our work and stand up and hold hands in a circle? Help. What is he up to? We're back to strange. I was just getting comfortable, and now, only the second day of class, I'm seriously doubting Professor Allender's grip on reality. Maybe he forgot this is a college class, not grade school. Apparently, I am not the only person who has doubts. I am hesitantly standing up, and I notice that everyone else has a quizzical look.

It's getting stranger. He just announced that we are going to do something extraordinary. We will learn the name of every person in the room after hearing it only once more. Right! I do know a few names already, but all the rest after hearing them only once? I wonder whether wacky activities are going to be the norm in this class. I will give him some credit though—for piquing my curiosity.

He's got our attention. This is what we have to do. We're going to play a game where we pass a pulse around the circle. Someone starts the pulse by squeezing the hand of the person next to them. It's a game I once played as a kid in summer camp. You wait for the person on one side of you to squeeze your hand, and as soon as he or she does, you squeeze the hand of the person on the other side of you. The pulse is passed on to the next person, who in turn passes it on. There is a new part though. Before you start the pulse going around, you say your name once, clearly. Then, you begin. As you wait for the pulse to get back to you, the whole class focuses the attention on just you. The task is to attach your name to an image of you in everyone's mind. Directing a little love and kind attention also helps. Cute. When the pulse gets back, you pass it to the person next to you again, and it is his or her turn.

Well, four people have taken their turn. So far, Professor Allender is right. Their names are clear as a bell. There are only twenty-five more to go. This is impossible. Still, it is interesting. It probably takes just a little more than thirty seconds for the pulse to go around. But, because we are staring at the person, it seems like an awfully long time. There is some squirming, a bit of giggling, but on the whole we are taking the activity seriously.

Nine down, and coming up to me. It's still working. I've got a clear picture of their names, and I assume overload is going to set in soon. The fact that I already know a few people's names, though, helps a lot. Whenever one of them is taking a turn, I don't have to focus my attention on that person. I only need to review the new names I've learned to this point. I've got fourteen.

My turn. Saying my name out loud with everybody paying attention to me certainly makes me feel important. I feel slightly embarrassed, but it doesn't feel bad. It's like getting complimented by someone in front of other people. It must be all that love they are focusing on me. How corny, and I like it. This really suits my shyness. I am the center of attention, and I don't have to say a word. This is much better than name games I've played in other classes. There, you get real nervous trying to figure out what priceless gem you are going to say about yourself and hardly hear any of the names before you speak. And even afterward most of the names go in one ear and out the other. Done. My turn is over, and I'm glad for that too.

While people were looking at me, I made special eye contact with those who had their turns before me. It is really clear to me that I know their names. I feel challenged. I've just learned four more. It's as if a lightbulb is going on over their heads. Better yet, it's a lighted sign with the name on it. Ten more to go, and, my luck, I already know two of these people's names for sure, and one I just need to confirm. This is weird. I *am* learning everyone's name. I've got four more, six to go. There is no question anymore that I'm going to know everyone's name. I'm on a roll.

I've got them! Professor Allender is asking if there is anyone willing to try and name each person in class. We're in a momentary lull, the kind I don't like. To my surprise, it's happening. My hand is going up. No surprise, he's calling on me.

Crystal?

I, I think I can name everyone.

Go for it.

Kwand . . . John . . . Steve . . . Sandy . . . Tiffany . . . Don . . . Mike . . . Leslie . . . Lauretta . . . Coleen . . . Michele . . . Jamie . . . Kim . . . me, Crystal . . . Tracy . . . Steve . . . Harry . . . Michele . . . Tracy . . . Prakash . . . Tony . . . Stacy . . . Cyle . . . Nicole . . . Shaari . . . Meredith . . . Joann . . . Carl . . . Suzy . . . Professor, uh, Jerry!

That's terrific! And, I'm comfortable with your using my first name. Let's give her a hand of applause. (Admiring applause.) Is there anyone else who can name everyone? Leslie. Mike. Great. I'm going to ask you to wait, though, until our next class to show off because we are running out of time.

In the time remaining, there are a few things I want to say. To begin with, I recognize that waiting until next week would seem to make the naming task harder. Trust me, it won't be. Your turn will come at the end of class, and by then you will have had more opportunities to relearn your classmates' names. The name list that I am going to hand out at the beginning of class next week will be particularly helpful. Not only for Leslie and Mike, it is meant to be useful for everyone else too. Even Crystal.

What have we learned in this last activity? Learning each other's names is not essentially different than memorizing any information. It is not magical. The task has been well begun, but it is hardly over. Those of us who know them already are likely to forget some. Those of you who don't know them all, that is, most of you, need to give up your sense of failing at the task and concentrate on how many names you did learn. All of us can take pride in the fact that we are way out ahead of what is likely to happen in other classes. One usually knows only a few classmates' names at the *end* of a semester!

Why, though, do we forget? All learning takes place in a context. Our learning here is mostly in the context of this large circle. You will be forming new groups for different activities. As you move around and change places, memory of each other's names will slip. We all share this difficulty, but, over time, we will get to know each other through a variety of experiences. These experiences will find special places in our minds, and then, all of a sudden, more and more people's names will be obvious to us in almost any context. After a few weeks, we will all comfortably know each other's names.

Our memories were assisted in many ways. The fact that we always knew the name of the person who was speaking in the discussion was an important element. On top of that, in the course of these two days, each of you had direct contact with a few people. Aside from anyone you met before or after class, there were your partners for discussing the syllabus; the teacher, for two minutes, who asked you a question; and the person who was your student. There were also several people whose names I kept forgetting. Having to ask again and again embarrassed me, and you saw that. Your efforts to help *me* helped *you* remember their names.

As to magic, Steve T. noticed a sleight-of-hand trick. On the first day, I insisted on collecting the information sheets with your names on them in the order you were sitting in the circle. People tend to sit in the same places. With this boost, by my example, I was able to make the possibility of your learning this many names seem more realistic.

All of these experiences acted as memory hooks. The pulse circle and the imagery activity acted as a powerful tool for consolidating this learning. For a few of you, it worked perfectly. That it didn't work as well for everyone points out that we all learn differently. The difficulties are the same for math, spelling, or vocabulary. Learning is tenuous at first and only becomes secure when it is approached from a variety of directions. This is what gives us flexible use of the knowledge. It is a common experience to discover that what one thought one knew cold becomes unavailable when taking a test.

Crystal here. What Jerry is saying makes sense, but it is too much for me to take in right now. I don't quite believe that I learned everyone's name, and I know I did. I am so pleased with myself, I feel giddy. There was a period there when I thought he wasn't playing with a full deck. It seems now to have been more than full, maybe stacked. What fascinates me is how learning can occur without being forced into my brain. It seems to have slipped in between the cracks when I wasn't noticing. I hope Jerry's creativity doesn't run out. I'll be more disappointed in this class than in one in which I am resigned to the boredom. We're not just talking about doing the first theme. So far, it is an effective learning environment. . . . (fade)

Before I dismiss class, I want to come back to the story about Trudy the bag lady and the two aliens. You can see that our main focus has not been on the readings. I don't mean to say that reading isn't important, no less than the play had to be a good one. Similarly, though, we will not be giving our primary attention to this knowledge. You can also see that I spent little time actively teaching. Readings, my teaching, and learning from each other are indeed an integral part of the process, but, in my biased view, it is your student and budding teacher selves, self-knowledge, that will give you the most relevant guidance.

Teaching about teaching is especially challenging because of the mirror that it creates. My job is to model effective teaching, and you can always see whether what I am doing fits with what I am saying. However, as happened this week, most of the attention will be focused on you—the audience.

(Back in my office) I'm reminded of when I was a kid doing magic shows for my friends. Their astonishment was so predictable. Now, every time I do this name memory trick, I get the same feeling. I want the central focus of my class to be on the students' improvisations, and yet, often, there are experiences that I set up for which the outcomes are predictable. This paradox is an important part of effective teaching.

I always like improving the show. It dawns on me that, as students arrive, I could put their names and an example of previous teaching experience on the board in a circle matching where they sit. For people who feel they have never taught, I could help them identify a time when they had an attitude of a teacher. Doing this would be preferable to waiting in silence until the official class time. I'll try this idea next semester. I bet the circle on the board will make learning names even easier. Maybe I could predict that everyone in class would know all the names by the end of the first week. That would really be a great trick!

3

Experience Experiments

Cast/Roll (in order of participation)

Jerry Allender:	Author, director, teacher
Tracy Burns:	Author, narrator, student
Donna:	Jerry's wife (not present)
Crystal:	Tracy's partner last week
Joann:	Tracy's partner this week
Kwand:	In Tracy's group of four
Meredith:	In Tracy's group of four
Cyle:	Discussant
Steve M.:	Discussant
Shaari:	Discussant

The opening scene finds the teacher in his office talking with a student on the telephone. It's Friday, still the first week. The office is a small room on the fourth floor of the Education Building, about eleven feet square, overfilled with four filing cabinets, three bookcases, a desk, and a small side table. There are four chairs in the center of the room, at odd angles, tucked in the little space left over and on the sill of a narrow window with a view of downtown Philadelphia in the distance, a tall leafy dieffenbachia.

The second and third scenes, in the seventh-floor classroom, take place the following Monday and Wednesday.

Hi Tracy. . . . Yes. I can arrange for you to be assigned to a different elementary school for your field placement. What's the problem? . . . I understand your concern about going into a tough neighborhood. Actually, though, the school you've chosen isn't really that far from campus. I would like you to go for your first scheduled time and then let me know how you feel. . . . True. . . . Other students coming from the suburbs have expressed similar feelings. Most of them did find that they were not uncomfortable once they got started. . . . Sure. If you continue to feel anxious, I'll be glad to find another school for you. . . . No problem, it's my job to be helpful. See you in class on Monday.

23

(There is a policy that students have to go their assigned schools. I think there should be some leeway. Most of the field placements are in public schools near the university, but the deteriorating neighborhood that surrounds us can feel very foreign. At the same time, though, I think that the challenge is reasonable.)

~

Last week, you were introducing yourselves to me. Today, I want to tell you a little about myself. I've pondered some of the reasons for how I teach. I remember never liking school. I also remember feeling smothered by the demands of teachers and not being a cooperative student. School seemed always to be getting in the way of my learning. Later, I did learn to be a good student; that's what got me to the place of being your teacher. Still, these lingering feelings have had a telling influence. I decided that I didn't want to teach the way I was taught.

Another important influence is my wife, Donna. When we met, I was a graduate student and she was a third-grade teacher. We have been talking about teaching now for over forty years. I appreciate the practical help that she gives. I tend to be theoretical. For all my ideas, without her down-to-earth common sense, I'm not so sure I would have become a skilled teacher.

One early memory, still vivid, is my telling her about a difficult day with two junior high boys who were misbehaving very badly. With words and my eyes, I had threatened them with physical force. Donna listened patiently. When I finished, she paused, looked *me* in the eye, and said, "Don't ever do that again." Besides it being wrong, she believed you just have to be much more clever to succeed as a teacher.

She and I have invented creative activities for each other's classes. We even have had some opportunities to teach together, and, altogether, it has been exciting learning for the both of us. Best of all, having someone to talk with regularly about teaching gave me a supportive and challenging environment in which growing and improving as a teacher were made easier. Because of this, I am motivated to provide a similarly safe and challenging environment for others who want to learn to teach.

(It's best to stop talking about myself here. Personal stories are appealing only to a point. Besides, the class seems eager to start working.)

I hope it is obvious that, as I have had influences, each of you has your own set as well. Your job is to develop a style of teaching that best fits how you have been influenced. Now, let's turn to the experience experiments.

The idea of the experience experiment is borrowed from the concept of pilot research that scientists use to initiate formal experiments. I learned in graduate school that there are no specific rules dictating how to carry out a pilot study. I was intrigued. The purpose is to find out the practicality of doing an experiment, and any approach that might lead to useful information is acceptable.

I realized that this is a way to test the practicality of new ideas in the classroom, a systematic way to improve. Once I got started, it wasn't long before the results began to have noticeable effects on my teaching. Every semester, I chose a special focus to explore: listening skills, student-directed teaching, imagery, role-playing, small groups, storytelling, and lots more.

Then, I adapted this learning strategy for a classroom assignment and named it an experience experiment. Briefly, take an idea from something you've read, or even from your imagination, think up a practical application, try it out with the students you teach, and describe what happened in a short paper. I find that if you use small intuitive steps, the results are likely to be positive. . . . (fade)

Hi, I'm Tracy Burns. I'm an elementary education major. Like most of the students here, this is my first education class. This is the second week, and, knock on wood, it seems like a good course. Although it's different, I like Professor Allender's method of teaching. He has spent only a little time lecturing, and even then he mostly likes to tell stories. He also seems to prefer to be called by his first name, but that's too informal for me—at least, just yet. I agree with Crystal, she was my partner last week, how she said he is sneaky. It's not mean, more in a nice sort of way. I keep wondering, What's going to happen next? So far, I'm looking forward to the rest of the semester.

I felt like such a whiner when I called to his office on the telephone at the end of last week. I was really uptight though. It was embarrassing for me to admit that I was scared to go to my assigned school. He was very considerate about how I felt, and even though I agreed to go anyway, at least once, I didn't feel bad or trapped into it when I finished talking with him. That meant a lot to me. It's so easy for teachers to ignore students' needs and how they feel. When I worry about how a teacher will treat me, it always brings up memories from when I was in third grade. The teacher constantly discouraged us from doing things in our own ways. Oddly, the worst memory is of something that actually happened to someone else. She humiliated one of my classmates because of the way he was holding his pencil. She kept taking his hand and forcing him to hold the pencil her way—the "right way"! I sometimes wonder how he holds his pencil now. Thinking about it still makes me angry.

I have a new partner today. After Professor Allender's short lecture, he put the titles of all seven books from which we've chosen on the blackboard. *Totto-chan* and *Growing Minds* specifically go with the first theme, but he asked us to read two chapters for this week from any of the seven to give us an overview of the whole course. I don't see what I'll get from other people's reading, but I am being patient. Up to this point, he's kept his promises. Anyway, after listing the books, he listed all of our names under the title of the book we had chosen and then paired us off with people who read the same book. I played it safe by choosing *Growing Minds* by Kohl so I wouldn't have two different books to read for the first few weeks. I am a little jealous of those who chose some of the later books. I'm curious. But I know eventually I'll get to them.

My partner, Joann, is telling me her reaction to the two chapters from Kohl's book that she read for this week. We've been asked to get to know each other and to share what we did for the first assignment. That's easy. The hard part is to listen carefully enough to remember what she is telling me. When we are finished sharing the assignment with each other, we are going to be joined with another group of two, who have also read Kohl's book for this week, and the task will be for each of us to introduce our partners to the foursome. Without assistance from Joann, I have to make a few personal remarks about her and then retell her experience experiment from beginning to end.

The activity is supposed to develop our listening skills. I don't have any argument with that. It turns out, though, that this is going to be another source of embarrassment for me. I really haven't taught anything in my classroom yet. There wasn't a chance to do an experience experiment. I was in the class once so far and only got introduced—to twenty-one sixth graders. I did the reading, and I wrote up the interactions with the children and my impressions. I am hoping Professor Allender will accept this for the assignment. I think he will, but I'm worried that the students in my group will think I'm flaky. Doing good work is important to me. It always bothers me when other students don't keep up.

(For a while, I was walking around, from pair to pair, briefly listening in on each conversation. I wanted to be sure that everyone understood the task. There have been times with this beginning activity, in other semesters, when students will keep on chatting and forget about the work I've asked them to do. No problem today. I'm sitting off to the side watching and listening to the sound level in the room. It usually is time to shift the task when their voices die off slightly.)

What Joann is telling me is interesting. She was asked to tutor a student, a first-grade boy, who was having difficulty reading. Her job was to help him with a lesson that he was supposed to be learning in class. His trouble was comprehension. The little boy is really a good kid, smart enough and lovable, but his attention span is very short. During the teacher's lesson, she was observing him and noticed how easily he became bored. When he loses his concentration, he starts drawing. Once, while the teacher was talking, Joann found herself poking him gently and telling him to sit up and listen. From reading Kohl, she wanted to emphasize the importance of teaching subjects in a way that all students can understand and, at their own pace, master. She decided to be less concerned with getting the whole lesson done on time. She focused on making sure that the boy was really comprehending the words that he was reading.

For her half-hour lesson, to keep the boy's interest, she also followed Kohl's idea of making the lesson fun and challenging at the same time. It's impressive what she came up with to help her student's learning. She started by making up a sentence of her own that made no sense. With small cards that all of the children had been asked to use to make up sentences, she deliberately constructed an incorrect sentence. The cards had individual words on them like *Sam, the, cap, at, mad,* and so on. It went something like, "The can Sam cap see," and then she read it out loud. The boy knew the sentence was wrong and looked at her like she was crazy. She told him that she was having trouble and needed his help to fix the sentence. He changed the words around until the sentence was right, and then, proudly, *he* read it out loud.

He was given five sentences, and he was able to do them all. The deliberate errors caught his attention. He was amused by Joann's silly mistakes. She felt, for a student who was behind the rest of the class, that it made him feel better to help his teacher with her sentences rather than having her help him.

Joann was pleased with her lesson, and so was I. This is an idea for teaching that I'm sure I'm going to use someday. It's my turn now to tell Joann about my *non*–experience experiment. I think I'll begin by telling her how good I feel in comparison with Kohl's description of his miserable, awful first job teaching. Children totally out of control walking all over him—that was my worst fantasy. I have to say that I was the luckier one. The teacher of my class was very nice. The children seemed to be in love with her. They showed respect, and they were, on the whole, well behaved. . . . (fade)

(It's time to move on to the second part of this activity. I need to check out whether there is any resistance. If anyone is in the middle of telling something especially meaningful to his or her partner, it's best, and fair, to give a few extra minutes to finish up. Either way, they do need to know that there is a goal out there that I want us to accomplish by the end of the week.)

Give me your attention for a minute. . . . Do any of you think that you will need five minutes more for sharing your experience experiments with each other? . . . No? Good. Take a minute to wind up your thoughts, and then I'll explain what happens next. . . . (fade)

Okay. On the board, I've listed the four people who will be in each group. Introduce your partner to the group and tell what happened in the experience experiment. Afterward, it's all right for him or her to add anything that makes the version of the story more accurate. Be sure to compliment your partner on the aspects of your work that were captured well in the retelling.

There is one final part to this task. You have to make a summary chart. Each group will be given colored marking pens and a large piece of newsprint. While you are listening, pay attention to the concepts from the readings that were used, what the lesson was about and how it was taught, and the results. When you have finished hearing from everyone, record the data that have been collected in the four experience experiments. Set up the chart with three columns and four rows, and assign each person a row. In the columns, summarize (1) the concept, (2) the lesson, and (3) the result. When the four experience experiments are brought together like this, the data will constitute a more formal piece of research. From our class, we will have seven charts, one from each group, and they will all be posted on the board across the front of the room for us to analyze.

On Wednesday, once the charts are done, we will use the data to answer and discuss one main question: How can an effective learning environment be created? This is the underlying question that you have been asking yourselves in each experience experiment. We will draw some general conclusions about the nature of an effective learning environment, and we will also have an overview of the coming semester's work. Any questions? . . . (fade)

(I'm fielding a few nervous questions. The summarizing task is not familiar ground. My concern is not to waste time regrouping into fours. Successfully leading activities like these depends on the students moving from one group to another without confusion. For young children, this would be called a transition time, and most elementary school teachers know very well that it must go smoothly. Once they are working on the task, I can help each group individually fill in its chart.)

Tracy here again. Kwand and Meredith joined Joann and me for our group of four. I think we may have spent a little too much time socializing at first, although Professor Allender didn't seem to mind. Or maybe when he came over and quietly stood listening for a few moments as he did with several other groups, he was subtly telling us to focus on our work. We're finally getting started. We agree that Kwand and Meredith will begin by introducing each other. . . . (fade)

It's helpful hearing what others did for their experience experiments. We're having a good discussion. Kwand was concerned about a spelling lesson matching his student's interests. He helped the student make up sentences for spelling words that had to do with his after-school activities. Meredith developed an arithmetic task for her student also using a card game, like Joann, but in a different way.

Knowing people's names is nice, and I am enjoying finding out other's reactions to the first assignment. I feel encouraged to get to know other students. It helps me break out of my shell. I am not as shy as Crystal, who told me last week about herself, but I usually don't open up unless I'm pushed. I'm actually doing a lot of talking in this class. I like sharing my thoughts and ideas with others in our little group. The discussion lets me realize that my ideas are not less valuable than other peoples', so I worry less that my ideas are stupid. I see that nobody can know, for sure, what approach will help a child's learning. Of one thing, I am sure. To be a good teacher, I have to develop more confidence in myself.

I also appreciate the discussion because it has given me some good ideas for the second experience experiment. Joann is going to introduce me next. . . . (fade)

It's Tracy again. I'm back. It's Wednesday, and Joann is recording our summaries on the chart for Kwand, Meredith, me, and herself. At the end of the last class, she did a great job retelling my first day's experience meeting the kids at my school. She hyped a bit what I told her, and it came out sounding like a really interesting story. I wasn't embarrassed at all for not having actually taught anything. In fact, Kwand and Meredith seemed almost jealous about the connections I established with the kids in such a short time.

The way Joann repeated what happened made the experience seem important. I loved how she dramatically conveyed my up and down feelings. 12:00. I arrive. I walk into the classroom ready for the worst. . . . No kids! They are at lunch. The teacher hardly introduces herself. The next thing you know I am grading math tests that were taken earlier in the day. I am disappointed to find that many of them have misspelled words on them. I find *thousand, hundred,* and even *twenty* misspelled. This really disturbs me, but at least the math problems are correct. This helps me realize that the spelling doesn't matter as much.

12:30. I'm still grading papers. . . . All of a sudden, the kids burst into the room. All at once, inquisitive children on four sides are bombarding me with questions. "What did I get on my test?" "Who are you?" "How long are you going to be here?" "Did I get a hundred?" "What's your name?" They are almost shouting, and they are expecting me to answer them. Not yet though. The teacher tells them to calm down and be seated. She introduces me, and then it is my turn to say a little bit about myself. Inside, I am terrified, but I don't show it. Usually, I am timid when speaking in front of people. This day is different. I am different. I stand in front of the class and speak, firmly, with authority. I tell them who I am, why I am there, and how I can help them.

The tougher part is next. The kids get to ask me questions. Ten hands go up at once. I choose an enthusiastic girl who is sitting in the middle of the room. She asks if they can call me by my first name. I see the teacher nod sideways ever so slightly, and a few students moan when I say no. More questions follow. Will I be coming only to their class? Do I like going to college? How is it to live in a dormitory? I answer them all without hesitation. I am delighted to feel so welcomed by them.

It is time for them to get ready for a spelling test, and I get ready to leave my first day in the classroom. As I am heading for the door, a few girls tell me to have a nice weekend and to have fun in my college classes. I tell them to do well on their spelling test and that I will see them next week. Just recalling the experience makes me feel good. I think Joann understood what happened better than I did. . . . (fade)

(Class is almost over. The charts are posted all around the room on the boards and the walls, and the room feels full of ideas. Awhile ago I gave them ten minutes to walk around and look at the charts. Combining the results from several experience experiments, most of the students easily came up with two or three generalizations about how to create an effective learning environment—though occasionally I had to push students to explain their concepts more carefully.)

I hate to interrupt the discussion, but I want to make a few closing remarks and give an assignment for next week. Our discussion of these summary charts has given us a great deal to think about. This is good work. You have identified useful concepts that are relevant to teaching and learning, and some of you have demonstrated an understanding of how these concepts can be applied practically.

Several comments stand out in my mind. I like how Cyle emphasized, from his reading of Kohl, the importance of not putting limitations on how much we think a student can learn. This open-ended attitude applies no less to ourselves than to those whom we teach. Students often ask whether one is born with the ability to teach. This question has no final answer. I do know, however, judging from where I started out, that we are not stuck with the skills we have when we begin teaching.

I appreciate Steve M. pointing to the connection he noticed between Linda Williams's book, *Teaching for the Two-Sided Mind*, and Maureen Mudock's book, *Spinning Inward*. In both, there is a focus on the uses of mental imagery in learning. Last week, you saw how I used an imagery technique to help us learn everyone's name. When we focus on the cognitive side of learning, we will read in *Teaching for the Two-Sided Mind* about a broad spectrum of ways in which the human mind functions, and we will see how imagery fits in. When we are working on the emotional side of learning, with help from *Spinning Inward*, we will explore how imagery can be used to expand students' learning potential.

Finally, I want to emphasize what Shaari said about *The Education of Little Tree* by Forrest Carter. This is a story, set in this century, about a young Native American boy who goes to live with his Cherokee grandparents in their isolated home in the mountains after his parents suddenly die. A moving book, it chronicles how this young boy learned what other children learn in school, and much more, without ever attending a school. It is important to notice how he is not protected from making mistakes. *The Education of Little Tree* opens our minds to a fresh view of how children can be encouraged to learn.

We've covered a lot this week, and I have one last question. Although it may be too early in the semester to ask, is there anyone who wants to share an insight that has come to you from your initial work in this class? . . . Tracy?

I have an insight that I am willing to share. It's a little embarrassing, but I want to tell it anyway. Before I went to my school for the first time, I felt afraid. I worried that I wouldn't be safe. I imagined that the children would almost always be out of control. As I was walking to the school, everything I was imagining was negative. Looking back on my feelings, I understand that my stereotypes had a strong effect on my expectations.

It turned out very different than what I expected. I realized that these kids aren't the badasses you read about in the newspaper or see on television. They are just kids. Curious, interested, and even pleasant. After reading about Kohl's awful first job, and looking back on my first day, I'm thankful that I was greeted so warmly by the children and the teacher. Similar to what Cyle said, I had held low expectations. I don't think that my stereotypes are totally gone, but I have changed some. Best of all, I look forward to going back to the school and having a chance to help teach the children some of their lessons.

That's quite an insight, Tracy. I'm reminded of a time when I was embarrassed by my stereotypes. I was telling Donna about the poor attitude of the jocks in one of my classes. This was another time she looked me in the eye. "I wonder," she said, "do all jocks look alike?" When I talked about them individually, she helped me see that each student has her or his special qualities.

4

Drawing Ideas

Cast/Roll (in order of appearance)

Jerry Allender:	Author, director, teacher
Tracy:	Member of Joann's group
Shaari:	Student whose name was forgotten four or five times
Joann Russo:	Author, narrator, student
Kwand:	Member of Joann's group
Meredith:	Member of Joann's group
Cyle:	Discussant
Kim:	Student lecturer
Michelle:	Discussant
Coleen:	Student lecturer
Mike:	Discussant
Don:	Discussant
Sandy:	Discussant

Both scenes are in the seventh-floor classroom. It's the third week of class, and as usual everyone is sitting in a circle. Class begins with the teacher telling the students about a few of his teaching experiences.

At the end of class last week, Tracy expressed some worry about embarrassing herself when telling us what happened the first time she went to her school to teach. When I was thinking about her experience over the weekend, I realized that the possibility of embarrassment and teaching go hand in hand. Difficult as it might seem, the possibility stares us in the face whenever we are in our classrooms.

I recommend that we all relax and recognize that embarrassment comes with the turf. Least bothersome for me is how I routinely embarrass myself when I am learning students' names during the first week. For example, I was most uncomfortable when I persisted in not knowing Shaari's name after the fourth or fifth

31

time she told me—in front of the whole class. But I tell myself that this kind of embarrassment is just a warm flush. Just as watching me turn red in the face helped you remember her name and the few others that I kept missing, the embarrassed feeling actually helps me too to remember people's names. The more embarrassed I get, the more likely I am to remember your name the next time you raise your hand to be called on.

The trick is not to become distressed about making mistakes. There is a natural desire to ignore or hide our mishaps. I find, though, that an honest awareness of mistakes and a willingness to let our students see them are much more fruitful. This lesson regularly reoccurs in teaching, and, if we're willing, there will be many opportunities to learn how to use mistakes to our advantage.

There is one experience, in particular, that I count among my most embarrassing moments. There is a slight risk that you might be disappointed with me once you hear about it, but I hope you will be understanding. I had been teaching in the College of Education for about ten years when a student confronted me with a difficult question, "Have you ever been a teacher?" I was afraid to answer the question directly.

Today, I can say that the answer is no, I have never had a regular teaching job in an elementary school, junior high, or high school, for a whole year, where I went to work from early morning to late afternoon. This may seem strange. How is it, then, that I believe that I can teach you about teaching? I've had many part-time positions, I've taught children of all ages, and I've been a teacher's assistant on many occasions. I also have had especially rewarding opportunities to team teach. You might say I've been an apprentice for forty years, and I never got further than a teacher's assistant. Think of me as a capable but slow learner.

On that day, ten years ago, when I didn't face this embarrassment, I hemmed and hawed. I wasn't willing for my students to see that I have a significant flaw. I have never done the real job that you will be asked to do. It wasn't intentional—a part of my educational plan. My career simply happened this way. The problem was that I turned it into a shameful secret. In spite of this flaw, I discovered that I am capable of teaching people how to teach children. Perhaps it is because of this lack of full-time teaching experience that I find it easy to empathize with the difficulties that you encounter in the development of your teaching skills.

A more regular source of embarrassment is tied to my discontent as a student. I promised myself that when I became a teacher I would teach differently than I was taught. Not knowing how, though, proved to be a big obstacle that felt almost insurmountable when I was starting out. Prior to becoming a college professor, in part-time teaching jobs, I had found some simple ways to teach creatively. However, I couldn't figure out how to apply these lessons to teaching about teaching.

I was giving lectures like everyone else and wondering if I had committed myself to a professional career that would bring me no end of disappointment. I was teaching the same way I was taught. To my credit, I soon stopped filling up class time with lectures. To the students' credit, they didn't flee from my classes. With only budding skills and a minimum of confidence, I insisted that most of my students' learning would depend on discussions—about what we read and our own ideas. For a long time, I think it was mostly sincerity that played the important role in my success. You can be sure that there were many awkward moments.

In thinking about the development of your own teaching skills, don't be discouraged. Over time, I have found that teaching has slowly become a little easier. I feel a little more graceful every year. Be aware, I don't intend for you to copy my style of teaching. Clearly, you have to figure out your own sense of what is meaningful teaching and learning. What we do have in common, though, is embarrassment. There is no way to become a better teacher without facing these kinds of feelings.

Let's turn back now to the charts from last week's experience experiments. Today, I want you to draw these ideas. Before I explain, let's review. . . . (fade)

I'm Joann Russo. I'm not planning to become a teacher, so you might imagine that I don't belong in this class. I wasn't sure myself at first. I'm a drama major, and I decided to take this course as an elective because I want to explore other career alternatives. Even though it's only our third week, I think the course is probably going to be helpful to me whether or not I end up changing my major to education. The professor wants us to relate what we are learning to our personal interests. Classes are very informal, many of us call him by his first name, and it's easy to participate in class discussions.

Jerry is doing most of the talking right now, but I don't feel like an outsider who is just being fed information. He starts each week by telling stories. I'm intrigued, and I appreciate his honesty. The stories have been interesting and often tie into my concerns. Also, I can see some connections with my drama studies. A lot of class time is spent in a circle discussing what we are learning, just as is done in acting classes. Something happens when people are sitting in a circle; it's like an unconscious communion. Answering questions and giving feedback are easier because the situation is relaxed and comfortable. And the ideas we have been discussing have pointed out ways that teachers have to act in order to help children learn. There is a kind of similarity between becoming an actress and becoming a teacher. As I'm not sure of what line of work I want to do, I'm especially glad that he encourages us to make our learning personally relevant.

I have to say, though, that asking us to draw is a little strange. We're just about to break up into the small groups we were working in last week, and I don't think I understand yet what we are supposed to do. Several students have asked how it is possible to draw the concepts from our experience experiments. Jerry is explaining that we can choose any focus. If we can't figure out how to directly illustrate a concept, it's all right to draw pictures of the lessons we taught the children. That's closer to something I understand. I used some of Kohl's ideas about how to challenge students. I haven't got any ideas for how to picture *chal-*

lenge, but I can imagine showing a first-grade student doing a lesson on word comprehension. At least, I could if I knew how to draw. I hope there is someone in my group who has artistic ability.

No one in my group—Tracy, Kwand, or Meredith—has asked any questions. Maybe they already have some good ideas for our drawing. Jerry told us when he first explained the assignment that, ideally, he wants each group to come up with a unified picture of our four experience experiments. That's a big challenge. I'm glad he is easy with us when we don't do exactly what he asks. He has already agreed, in answer to Cyle's question, that, if we get stumped, we can combine four separate drawings into the same picture. I have no problem with the assignment as a whole. We're supposed to make a visual aid for a lecture on creating an effective learning environment. Doesn't sound so difficult. It's the details that are getting in my way.

I forgot to mention that he also made another one of his weird predictions. He said that seven of us, one from each of the small groups, are going to take part in giving this lecture, to this class, this coming Wednesday. Then he said the same thing he told us about learning everyone's name in class by the end of the first week—it would be effortless. We shouldn't worry because those of us who will do the lecturing will manage easily. I'll try not to worry, but just the thought makes me nervous. I'm a very talkative student. It's hard for a teacher not to notice me. I wouldn't be surprised if I'm one of the students he picks. Oh well, there is nothing I can do about it now, and he did make good on his prediction about my learning everyone's name with little effort. . . . (fade)

(It's at this point that I do a little bluffing. I have a vague worry about the assignment going awry. The obstacle we are facing, however, is not the prediction on how well their lecturing will go but, rather, getting to that point. I have never completely figured out how to explain to students the notion of drawing an idea. Mainly, my strategy is to stimulate courage for trying. I'll give a couple of examples of pictures I might draw and then push and pull some while they are working on theirs.)

You don't need to be so afraid of this drawing assignment. Simple pictures or diagrams will be perfectly adequate. Or, if you choose to draw your students with you teaching them a lesson, and you don't feel comfortable with your artistic ability, use stick figures.

For example, if I wanted to illustrate the main learning concept behind the activities we started doing in this class last week and are continuing now, I would draw a picture of a scaffold, the kind that builders use for construction. We have been following the necessary steps for planning an interesting lecture. First, we organized ideas and applications into summary charts, and now we are planning visual aids. The results of these activities are the scaffold that will enable you to stand up in front of the class and do only one thing—talk about what you've learned by explaining your charts and drawings. Without the scaffold, you would have to do all of the preparation on your own. There would be much more to worry about and more chance of failing. When all this work is done, doing your part of the lecture will be relatively easy. The scaffold doesn't insure success, but it does greatly increase the probabilities.

Another example might be to illustrate how our class will be set up for the lecture this coming Wednesday. At the top of the picture, toward the left, I'd put seven rectangles in a row to represent the two-by-three-foot newsprint concept charts from last week. Across from these, on the top toward the right, I'd put a row of seven more rectangles to represent the seven newsprints you are drawing this week. I would arrange all fourteen of the rectangles on a slight curve and make it look like they were hung on the large blackboard that runs across the front of our classroom. Across the bottom, there would be two rows of small circles to represent the students in this class—facing the newsprints above. In the middle, I'd place one more small circle with a T in it for the teacher. Finally, I would mark a T in seven of the small circles to represent the students, one from each group, who will also be lecturing, plus connecting arrows showing them replacing me.

Unless there is some other pressing unanswered question, I want you to go ahead and reform the groups of four that you worked in last week. Start by discussing what kind of drawing you think you could do to represent your concepts and experience experiments. If you are still worried, remember what I said a few moments ago. You only need fear a little embarrassment—which is what we are learning to overcome. Ready to work? . . . Good. Time to regroup. . . . (fade)

At this point, Kwand, Meredith, Tracy, and I have been talking about different possible drawings for about a half hour. We aren't exactly arguing. We have been struggling though, and to put it mildly, the discussion has been very energetic. We've laughed a lot too, and I'm hopeful that we will come to some decision soon.

At the beginning of the discussion, we all easily agreed that we needed to make our concepts appear interesting because that was how they affected us and our students. Using this basic idea, Meredith and I had organized our teaching as demonstrations and had made up games using cards. It was fun for both of our students, and they became naturally interested in what they were learning. Kwand had taken a more traditional approach by having his student simply make up sentences for helping him to learn words for a spelling test. But with his thoughtful encouragement, the sentences expressed the student's own special interests, and that tied, Kwand pointed out, our three experience experiments together.

I felt badly that Tracy might be left out because she hadn't had a chance to teach anyone yet. Meredith noticed, though, that the way in which Tracy introduced herself to her students also connected with our main concept. How she led a discussion with her students completely captured their interests.

Some frustrating moments followed next. We felt we had a theme without creative ideas for drawing it. Nobody could come up with suggestions for how to picture our combined concept of needing to interest students in their learning. Tracy got really annoyed. She said that she hated drawing and that, if she wanted to be an art major, she wouldn't be in this class. It didn't help when Meredith and I said that we didn't feel comfortable drawing either. Thank God for Kwand, who, admitting he was no great artist, said he could manage stick figures and diagrams.

There were a few moments of silence, which Tracy interrupted with the welcome suggestion that we try brainstorming. We all started talking at once with a bunch of really silly ideas. They didn't solve our problem, but it sure was fun. I wanted us to draw a skyscraper with huge neon billboards advertising our lessons. Everyone squashed my idea. They said the newsprint wasn't tall enough. Frankly, I think they were still being silly. Tracy suggested showing a regular classroom in which we would picture all of our lessons going on at the same time. This was rejected by Kwand, who felt it would be too hard for him to draw.

We have pretty much given up on drawing a general concept, and we are agreeing that we want to have something that represents our four individual lessons in one visual aid. Meredith is suggesting that we put pairs of stick figures, one for the student and one for the teacher, in their own area of the newsprint and somehow show ourselves each teaching our different lessons. I like this idea. I just added the possibility of putting rows of little circles, which Jerry suggested, for Tracy's lesson because that would show a whole class of students for her. I think we've almost got it. Tracy wants us to put two faces at the top of the picture. One would be frowning, with a question mark in a balloon coming out of its head. The other would be smiling under a balloon with a lightbulb in it. The faces will represent, before and after, how our students really learned their lessons.

Great! I think a lightbulb is going on above the heads of our group. We're going to draw cards in front of Meredith's student and mine. Hers will have math problems on them, and mine will have simple words that could be a comprehension lesson. In one hand of Kwand's student, there will be a piece of paper with a spelling list on it. The stick figure of Tracy will show her talking in front of her class. I don't think Kwand feels that he will have any trouble doing this drawing. He's already starting to draw the frowning face at the top of the picture. . . . (fade)

~

(With only a little resistance, all of the groups got started on their drawings last Monday, and today not much time will be needed to complete them. What intrigues me is how enthusiastic the students are about what they have accomplished—even though the drawings are basically quite simple. Their enthusiasm is another element that is predictable. It seems to naturally accompany assignments that encourage creativity. The challenge for me is to corral the expression of this energy in ways that meaningfully lead to my goals and theirs.)

Before starting today's lecture, there are several jobs that need to get done. You'll have a few moments to put the finishing touches on your drawings. Those of you who finish first, post the newsprints and set up the chairs the way I described on Monday.

First though, we have to choose the people who are going to lecture with me. The method involves a short imagery activity that combines the interests of others choosing you and you choosing yourself. Know at the outset that no one has to teach with me today who doesn't want to. Now, close your eyes and get a picture of someone in the group, yourself or someone else, standing in front of the class explaining the chart and the drawing. Hold the image in your mind for a moment. Has everyone got a picture? . . . Great. Now open your eyes and share your images with each other. . . . (fade)

Joann here again. I know I said that I appreciate Jerry's honesty, but I too have to say he can be sneaky. Guess who is doing the lecturing for our group. Me. I'm not surprised that Tracy imaged me, but Kwand and Meredith did too. I had Kwand in mind. To tell the truth, though, I wanted to image myself. It would have been normal for me to resist politely, but I didn't have a chance. They said that I was a natural because I was so talkative. Jerry's imagery activities are tricky. They help you see things in a different way. Even though I'm a little scared, I'm actually excited that I'll get to do the lecturing for my group. . . . (fade)

As I assured you, the people who have agreed to lecture don't have to worry. Your job will be easy. Listen carefully to the person who lectures just before you do. Then, all you need to do is to take that person's place standing up here and talk about the summary chart and your drawing. Try to connect your ideas with previous ones that were covered, but it isn't essential. When you are finished explaining your newsprints, ask for questions and comments. The rest of you should try to be your best student selves and make it as easy as possible for the teacher to succeed. Remember, you'll have your turn up here, if not today, another day soon. Don't be shy about participating in the discussion. If there is a big lull, I'll help out.

I'll introduce the lecture with some of the concepts we have been discussing and a few new ones. We have been building a scaffold together as a support for talking in front of a whole class of students. The scaffold has two interrelated functions. The first is to provide safe conditions for doing something untried and different. The second is to create a situation that feels challenging. As you are listening to the lecture, watch for other examples of scaffolding that naturally occurred in the lessons you prepared and taught your students. If the person lecturing doesn't mention them, point them out when he or she asks for comments. For the discussion after the lecture, I hope we'll have some good ideas for how scaffolds can be built for teaching reading, writing, and math.

Another focus has been on imagery. Sometimes, the emphasis is on images we hold in our minds. Other times, we translate these images into drawings and other artistic forms. I emphasize imagery because it is helpful for creating new ideas and breaking mental sets. I think of it as a way of making spaces in the mind for new learning. Visual expression in school usually takes a backseat to our concerns for verbal knowledge. Yet, from my experience and my research, I have found that it is an important tool that can be used to facilitate children's learning and our own. At the end of this lecture, we will compare the ways in which the use of imagery has already been helpful for your learning in this class.

Finally, I want to point out how this week's lesson is structured. The activities provide experiential work that implicitly has both freedoms and boundaries. If the freedoms interest and involve you, there is a tendency for you to accept the limitations that I set. I have to be constantly sensitive to whether the work I am requiring taps into your real interests. At the same time, I have to be careful that the level of difficulty I create makes it likely that the large majority of what is accomplished is just as acceptable to me. I find that under these conditions, students of all ages are more than ready to cooperate, and we both accomplish our goals. Discipline problems develop when these conditions don't exist. We'll talk more about this aspect next week. For now, concentrate on how these ideas, and the ones you are about to hear, can be applied to your own teaching.

Okay, Kim, you pick up the lecture from here. . . . (fade)

(The students' lectures are going all right. They find it easy to explain the work that their groups did. They mostly need support from me when it comes time for the discussion. If the silence lasts for more than about ten seconds, I ask a question or make a comment myself. The general mood, though, is energetic, and many of the students have been eager to get involved. There were even long periods during which I wasn't in the discussion at all. Everyone was focused on the student who was teaching. I like it when this happens. It's a good example of student-directed learning.)

(Joann) The end of the lecture is in sight. I know because I'm going to be last. Listening to everyone else and having to wait hasn't helped my nervousness, but it could have been worse. The drawings and the ideas that have been explained are intriguing. The discussion has been very active—which has kept me from worrying too much.

Kim mentioned the two books we haven't talked about yet—*Freedom to Learn* and *Emerging as a Teacher*. They sound really interesting to me. The first book is an idealistic philosophy of education by Carl Rogers and Jerome Freiberg which is supposed to get us thinking about our own ideal theory of teaching. The second one, by Robert Bullough, Gary Knowles, and Nedra Crow, is based on real-life stories of six first-year teachers, three of whom succeeded and three who will probably quit teaching. For our last reading of the semester, per usual, we have to choose one of the two books. It's going to be a hard decision—unless I decide to read both of them.

Starting with Kim, and since then, there has been a barrage of concepts, applications, and pictures. I like looking at the drawings. There is a tree with roots, a sky with stars, an artist's palette, a kindergarten classroom, and everywhere, stick-figure children and teachers. It's a grand display of colorful images of growing and learning. For me, the drawings show the high energy and fun that can be a part of helping others learn. I did have some good teachers in grade school and high school, but I wish more of my learning experiences, even in college, were like this.

It's my turn to lecture. . . . (fade)

That wasn't too bad. Judging from my own feelings, the students' participation in the discussion, and Jerry's smile when I was sitting down, I actually think I did a good job. I started out by mentioning the concepts we had covered so far that were new for me and how much they had captured my interest. I told the class that needing to interest students in their learning was our central concept. The transition felt very natural. Then, I summarized the concepts that our group used and told how each one of us had done the experience experiment.

The drawing was the easiest part to explain. I simply pointed out which stick-figure pair went with which experience experiment. The little circles for students in Tracy's class and the meaning of the frowning and smiling faces at the top were obvious to everyone. The discussion got going even before I asked for questions and comments. A couple of people wanted to know more details about our lessons, and there were some comments about Tracy's discussion with her students. Michele thought our two faces show how there often is a special moment when learning just happens. One minute you don't have it, the next you do. Her comment was thought provoking. I had fun teaching the class, but I'm still glad my turn is over. . . . (fade)

I enjoyed hearing each of you lecture. It is rewarding to me as a teacher when students do such good work. Coleen's ideas about a learning environment that encourages students to act naturally, based on Kuroyanagi's book *Totto-Chan*, give us a better understanding of what happened in class today. All you had to do was improvise with what you already knew within the scaffold that we collaboratively created.

Now it's time for the concluding discussion. The students in the front row stand up and turn your chairs around so that you face the row behind, and we'll have our regular circle. . . . As a guide for this discussion, I want you to recall the three questions that I asked earlier. Who remembers well enough to restate them? I'd appreciate a brave volunteer. . . . Go ahead, Joann.

The first one had to do with finding examples of scaffolding in the experience experiments. The second one was about the effect of imagery activities on our learning. The last one had to do with freedom and limits, which you just mentioned again in connection with *Totto-Chan*.

Well said. Joann, if you were leading the discussion, what question would you start with?

. . . Did anyone notice examples of scaffolding when we were discussing the experience experiments?

Would you be willing to lead the discussion for a while starting with that question?

. . . Okay.

Great. I have to leave class for a short while. You take over. I'll be back in ten or fifteen minutes. . . . (fade)

Me and my big mouth. I knew I would get chosen, but I was so sure my turn was over. You can never be sure what is going to happen next in this class. Well, the discussion is finally off and running. It wasn't so easy, though, getting it started.

At first, being put on the spot made me unsure of myself. I nervously repeated the question about scaffolding, and not one hand went up. My face probably turned bright red. As I was looking out at everyone in the circle, the students seemed to be staring at me and waiting for *me* to say something else. At that moment, although I had already become very comfortable in this class and friendly with my classmates, suddenly they were strangers. I hesitated, but then I said to myself that Professor Allender made me a teacher so I better conduct myself like a teacher and get this discussion going!

Because he regularly leads this kind of summary at the end of almost every class, I felt basically familiar with his style. He either proposes a question or asks if anyone wants to comment on something. I like having these discussions because they are a good opportunity to get information about what other students are thinking and doing. If you are having any problems, Jerry is often helpful himself, but mostly he encourages other students to offer their opinions. For instance, last week Tracy brought up her initial fears about how she would manage in her field placement, and I had similar feelings. It was comforting to know that I wasn't the only one. She was given good advice by other students as well as Jerry, and I felt it applied to me too.

Sitting there, slightly stunned, I reminded myself that I am a drama major who has had plenty of experience improvising. I sat up straighter and hoped that the second question would work. I asked if anyone had noticed examples of imagery. Mike commented, and then no one else. Silence. This time I didn't get nervous. Instead, I did what Jerry always does. Rather than pushing the question and begging people to respond, I just moved on immediately to the next question.

And that's when my creativity kicked in. I decided to make the question as personal as possible. I asked them, What have you learned about freedom and limits from being a student in this class? This question got their attention. Don responded energetically with a story from his elementary school that was a good comparison. No one responded again, so I told a short story from my experience that was similar to Don's. Sandy jumped in with a question about an experience of hers in high school, and since then it's been one question, comment, or opinion after another. The main thing I'm doing is nodding to people to speak when someone's hand goes up asking for a turn.

Jerry just walked back in the room and sat down in an empty seat in the circle. No one is paying any attention to him. It's as if they are too involved in the discussion to notice. It's just like the story I heard in an acting class the other day. A great actor was asked about playing the role of King Lear. He said, "I'm not *playing* King Lear, I *am* King Lear!" That's me. I *am* the teacher! Wow! I love this.

Joann, I apologize for interrupting this terrific discussion you are leading. There are only five minutes left before class is over, and I need to clarify next week's assignment.

That's all right, Jerry, but you have to wait until Henry has had a chance to comment. He's been waiting for his turn practically since the discussion began. . . . (fade)

5

Role-Playing

Cast/Roll (in order of appearance)

Steve Trois:	Author of the spaceship story and a member of Shaari's group
Jerry Allender:	Author, director, teacher
Shaari Mersack:	Author, narrator, student
Tiffany:	Member of Shaari's group
Steve M.:	Member of Shaari's group
Crystal:	Member of Shaari's group
Jamie:	Member of Shaari's group
Henry:	Last volunteer 1
Don:	Last volunteer 2

The opening science fiction short story, written for a final paper, takes place on a spaceship about 1,000 years in the future. The other two scenes, Monday and Wednesday, are in the regular classroom in the Education Building.

~

The desk felt cold and hard beneath my damp palms. The polished laminated surface flashed the reflection of the ceiling lights in my eyes. I started around the desk.

In the back of the room, there were two disruptive students. Yes, we had talked theoretically in my teacher education classes all about what to do with students like this, but this was real. There were no rehearsals and no retakes now. My mind was racing with the first step that I took toward them. It was full with all of the possibilities discussed in class about situations just like this one. Should I stand up straight and make myself look military? Command them to pay attention with a cold piercing glance? No, that's not the way. There is too little action in that plan. This situation calls for sterner stuff.

Could turning the lights on and off be a solution? All I would have to do is make a quick left turn and, then, only five steps to the wall. Would that work?

43

Do I have enough time? No, it's too dramatic. I could try for a position between the class and the disruption and make myself a human lighting rod channeling the excess negative energy away from everyone else. I had observed a class in which a teacher had done this. One student was dragging another out of the room, and the teacher still managed to keep the peace—moving very swiftly. Now, a second step. My left foot pressed into the ersatz marble tile. If I reached them soon, my authoritative teacher presence would defuse the conflict and the tension.

The noise in the classroom seemed to increase with every micron I moved. Do they sense the titanic struggle of wills that is about to commence? Could it be the Doppler effect, in the confined classroom stale air, channeling and increasing the noise as I move closer?

Cold sweat appeared on my now furrowed brow. My third step took me gracefully around the desk placing me on a collision course. In my path was a round metal cylinder full of waste papers—turned in by these very students and discarded because they didn't make the grade. My right toe came in contact with the can as I tried without success to skirt it. I heard the can screech across the floor making a sound like fingernails on an old-fashioned blackboard.

My blood boiled. Goose bumps erupted on my skin. My face turned red as the elevation of my blood pressure rapidly turned the goose bumps back into flesh. I heard the tremendous clang of the can slamming into a student's desk. Papers strewed themselves on the floor like forgotten autumn leaves. The can, rolling over several times, made a hollow ringing sound and then suddenly stopped. The room was conspicuously quiet.

At that moment, the bell rang. A rush of bodies scurried past me. They were abandoning the diminishing safety of the classroom for the dangerous but hopeful uncertainty of the hallways. They were gone, vanished, and I, left here with my frustration, doubts, and rage echoing hollowly in my head. Alone.

Professor Allender touched my shoulder with the power and firmness of an aikido hold. His sonorous voice reached my ears. "Stephen, your role-playing the teacher was good. Next time, though, try to play the role with a little less enthusiasm."

I sat for a few minutes and pondered, reflected. What is my idea of a teacher? The answers came from the silent walls. My reflection shone on their dull matte finish. I must teach with my heart and soul the essence of myself. The classes and tests are designed to explore new worlds—inside me and inside my students. I don't need to travel the universe to look for new lessons and new techniques. Being a teacher is as close as myself.

I got up and said, "Computer, end program." The classroom scene faded away into the black square room with the yellow grids etched on its four walls, floor, and ceiling. The doors slid open, and I walked out of the hologram simulator to go to my next class.

Well, it's Monday, and I am ready for another strange afternoon in Jerry Allender's class. I'm Shaari Mersack. Jerry is one of my first education teachers. Even though this is my junior year, I just transferred into the College of Education. University hasn't been easy for me, but at least now I'm finally decided about why I'm here. I realize that I want to be a teacher. Typically, I think of myself as a traditional student. It's ironic because this is the most unconventional class I have ever been in, and I love it. I'm getting a chance to understand myself better, which is what I need.

We're going to do role-playing today. I don't know much about role-playing, so I'm not exactly sure where it will fit in. The plan, though, seems simple enough. In a few minutes, the class is going to be broken up into groups of six according to the first book we chose to read. My book, *Totto-chan*, is the one about the little first-grade Japanese girl who was expelled from school because she didn't pay attention. I wanted to read about the new school that her mother found where children's individual needs are specially considered.

Our assignment is to identify a few passages in the book that we think are important. Once we've chosen the passages, we're supposed to help each other plan a ten-minute lesson. Then, we'll each get a turn teaching the lesson to our small group. Jerry warned us not to put off volunteering for our turns because the role-playing is going to be easiest at first. The difficulty is going to be regularly increased, and the challenge will be hardest for those who go last. I'm torn. I don't want to go first, and I don't want my turn to be too hard.

He hasn't fully explained yet what we'll actually be doing. He's still in the middle of a story about how he is learning to play jazz trumpet. Sometimes, I feel that this class is a mystery. . . . (fade)

Three years ago, I decided to pick up my trumpet again. I had been in a high school band, but that was concert music. I wanted to play jazz. Of course, no musician's life is complete without a downfall. The snag, ironically, was the encouragement I was getting as a beginner. People enjoyed how I played slow, relatively easy ballads. But it wasn't long before the music got more complicated. Paying little attention to self-doubts worked best, so when asked, I always said I could play whatever tunes came up. The importance of believing in myself—saying over and over in my mind how I'm a competent horn player—came out of research on mental imagery.

Then there was the night the bubble burst. Friends who were playing at a downtown restaurant asked me to sit in on a couple of songs. On the second number, I came in measures late and ended a long way before the tune ended. They weren't too hard on me, but I was very embarrassed. The hardest part was that when they gave me advice on how to improve, I didn't have a clue about how to apply it. I had no knowledge of how the skill of improvising is actually developed.

I found a jazz trumpeter who would teach me. I learned a lot—theory about the structure of jazz, plus greater range, more speed, and an improved sound.

However, hearing the structure as it is happening, the notes, the chords, and the rhythm, continued to elude me. When I was lucky, I played beautifully. When I lost the structure, I felt hopeless. My teacher didn't know how to help me, and I quit my lessons.

Deep down, I felt capable of learning. I talked about my feelings with musician friends, and that's how I met my second teacher. He taught elementary school music with an approach to teaching that complemented mine. He carefully adapts what his students learn to their interests and abilities. We came up with the idea of studying music with him the way he teaches children. In talking about my frustration, it became clear that I had missed some basic learning about music in my early lessons as a child. With the usual emphasis on performing and not making mistakes, I hadn't been encouraged to tap into my individual strengths, nor had there been opportunities to be playful with music. This is where we began.

He introduced me to a simple scale—just five notes. For several months, I only played C, D, E, G, and A. That's all. I spent hours making up melodies with these few notes. It's amazing how many combinations and rhythms are possible. I sang them and played them on the trumpet, the recorder, and the piano. We focused on variations—long notes, short ones, repeated, many, few, or not even there, rests. The melodies hovered on some of the five notes or all of them. They went up, down, up and down, down and up, straight for a while, and in all manner of patterns.

It was child's play, it was improvising, but I was doing it with a sense of control. Feeling in control is the key. I was learning about the spontaneous creation of music within a structure. I graduated to a simple folk song that also uses only five notes. Recently, I learned to play the song happily, sadly, with many variations, as a folk song, as a march, as classical music, as a rag, and just the other day, as jazz. None of it is very complicated. I still feel frustrated when the variations don't come easily, but mostly I enjoy learning and am making good progress.

Besides the fun of the music, I discovered that these experiences helped my teaching—which is why I am telling you this story. My experiences have put me more firmly in touch with my student self. You have heard me emphasize the need to develop our teacher selves. To do that well, though, requires constantly remembering what it feels like to be a student. I think that teachers are kept honest by regularly involving themselves in new learning.

Even more surprising, this new learning showed me how a teacher's task is similar to that of a musician's—to create a comfortable structure within which it is possible to interact with students spontaneously. The structure, through readings, fieldwork, and activities, conveys ideas, concepts, practical experience, and, of great importance, the boundaries that define the learning environment. If the teacher is then responsive to the ongoing changing conditions in the classroom, with the structure in place, it is possible for teaching and learning to be especially lively. The likelihood of teacher's and students' strengths surfacing is greater, as is meeting each of their needs. I feel that my musical learning has given me a more spirited sense of alternatives, not only when I'm playing trumpet but when I'm teaching too.

This leads us to today's role-playing. I'm going to define the boundaries for a short teaching experience, and your job will be to come up with some alternative ways you might act in this situation. Before forming groups of six, there are three questions to answer: What, who, and how are you going to teach? For the *what*, in a give-and-take discussion, the group should choose anywhere from one to six short passages from your book for planning a ten-minute lesson. If you all agree on one, great. If you can't agree, choose as many more passages as you need until everyone in the group thinks that he or she has meaningful ideas to teach. The *who* is easy. The members of your group will be your students. Each of you will get a turn teaching a lesson to five others.

Finally, *how*? I want you to imitate the most figural teacher described in the book you read. For *Growing Minds*, it is the author, Herbert Kohl. For *Totto-chan*, it is the headmaster, Mr. Kobayashi. Ask yourself how this person would teach your lesson. Imagine attitudes as well as specific behaviors. Then, try to model your teaching as closely as you can to your images. In a nutshell, you are going to teach your book, to your group, in the style of the book's main teacher.

This defines the first two rounds of role-playing. Work together for a while on the task as a group. As soon as two in each group get a handle on this lesson, I want you to volunteer to be the first teachers. These people will come out in the hall with me for a teachers' meeting while the others continue working. We'll talk about your plans, and I'll give some advice. One at a time, when you're ready, each of you will take a turn teaching your group. You start the role-playing by saying, "Begin," and if time doesn't run out first, you can stop anytime by saying, "End." When the first two rounds are finished, we'll reconvene the whole class for a discussion before going on to the next turns. For now, the rest of you will play your normal student selves. Later, the students will also have defined roles, but not yet.

Okay, form the small groups. Start working, and I'll come around to each group and answer questions. . . . (fade)

(Although some of the students feel nervous about this activity, the roles they'll play today won't be hard to manage. It's not easy to actually create the feel of Kohl or Kobayashi as we have gotten to know them from our reading, but the students who volunteer for this first round are, at least, likely to behave somewhat differently than they normally expect of themselves. This will be sufficient to give us something to think about and will be a good introduction to role-playing. What I need mostly is their confidence for trying out new behaviors— which will be especially important in the next rounds when *their* students won't be playing their usual compliant roles.)

(Shaari) It's Wednesday. I'm still a little nervous, but I'm looking forward to more role-playing today. Steve T. and Tiffany were the teachers at the end of Monday's class. That leaves Steve M., Crystal, Jamie, and me for today. It didn't seem so difficult. I wonder what changes will make it harder.

Actually, planning the role-playing was the most interesting part. We really got into a good discussion of *Totto-chan*. I wasn't surprised. It reads like a novel. By the time I was halfway through, I couldn't put it down. For sure, this was more fun than reading a textbook. It was amazing to think about how long the headmaster listened to Totto-chan the first morning she first came to the Tomoe school. I suggested that we build the lesson around the story of how Mr. Kobayashi kept asking her if there was anything else she wanted to talk about—from morning until it was time for lunch.

Everyone agreed that the value of listening carefully to students was the important lesson. Steve M., though, thought we ought to teach more than just one concept. Tiffany felt the same way. She didn't want to leave out mentioning the list of choices that was put on the blackboard every morning. Allowing students to choose the order in which they learn each subject, according to their interests, is something she had never experienced in school. It was much the same for the rest of us, and Steve and Crystal supported using Tiffany's idea. Nobody disagreed. Then our excitement mounted, and we started throwing in a bunch of other ideas all at once, one on top of the next, so you couldn't tell which was which. Jamie got exasperated and said that if we included all these ideas, we would be trying to teach half of the book in ten minutes.

We finally settled on using the first two ideas and one more from the book's introduction. Mr. Kobayashi told teachers that children shouldn't be fit into preconceived molds: "Don't cramp their ambitions. Their dreams are bigger than yours." He talked about the harm done by labeling or humiliating children because they are different. He mostly wanted teachers to help children find their individual strengths. We decided to use these three passages for our lessons. On Monday, Steve T. and Tiffany's lessons were the same, but their emphasis wasn't, so I think it's going to be interesting again today.

As to imitating Mr. Kobayashi, I'd give Steve a 7 and Tiffany about a 5. They both let us choose which passage we would use to begin the discussion, and they listened very carefully to every student's viewpoint. When I spoke, their reactions helped me to feel that what I was saying was important. And they certainly didn't label or humiliate anyone. It seemed, though, that they were mainly playing themselves.

In the class discussion afterwards, Jerry didn't think this was a problem—even when Steve added a question about the development of children's imaginations while passing around a stuffed animal belonging to his young daughter that he happened to have in his knapsack. It really wasn't that far from the kind of thing Mr. Kobayashi would have done. Jerry observed that everyone did the role-playing more than adequately well. He wasn't looking for us to become good actors.

He had mainly hoped we would become comfortable teaching with less focus on our egos. This seemed to work for Steve and Tiffany. . . . (fade)

Crystal and Jamie are now in the hall at the teachers' meeting. We're waiting for one of them to come back to role-play our teacher. Boy, this is going to be different than the last two times! Jerry warned us, and he says it's going to get harder yet. I wish I had done my teaching in the first round or at least in this one. I blew it. I didn't volunteer on Monday, and this time I hesitated, and Crystal and Jamie got chosen. Oh well, we're having too much fun planning our student roles for me to worry about it.

After the teachers went out in the hall for their meeting, Jerry came back for a minute to tell us that our task was to plan special student roles for ourselves. We had to come up with four ways in which students complicate the life of the classroom and then figure out how we could each act like one of these students. For the role-playing to work, he stressed, several times, the need to balance positive and negative behaviors, but I don't think anyone is listening. We are going to be *bad*! I'm going to be the student who is always talking. Tiffany will be disinterested. Steve T. doesn't want to follow directions, and Steve M. is going to be mischievous. Both guys want to make the teacher very miserable, and I don't think either of us women is going to be much better. I do feel sorry for Crystal and Jamie, and we haven't stopped laughing since we started planning.

The teachers and Jerry are coming back in the room. . . . (fade)

Okay, quiet down. Remember, before the role-playing gets under way, the teacher for each group sets the scene. When ready, he or she will say, "Begin." Wait a minute though because I have to make a couple comments.

Everyone has a role to play. The goal is to discover what kinds of alternative possibilities emerge in this real but unreal situation. Recognize that you are safe enough because, bottom line, we are all in the same boat and need to be supportive of each other. However, it is no longer a sure thing that you will succeed in your roles. This is where the challenge comes in.

Think of this as an opportunity to try out new kinds of behaviors. Often in life, the expression of our voices is inhibited by our worries. When we give in too easily, we can lose parts of our honesty, our creativity, and even our rights. This is what a lack of empowerment is about. On the flip side are actions that get us what we want. In the classroom, the trick is to not get locked into thinking about our teacher selves in a single rigid way. As anywhere, we have many potential selves that are ready to be expressed. This is the jazz part. Of course, we can't expect every alternative we come up with to work. Some of them might even feel phony. But this is a place to invent and try out new possibilities. It is a helpful way to expand our teaching skills. As to the student roles, I think they are important, too, because they help us empathize with students' needs. More on this later.

After the next two teachers have had their turns, instead of meeting as a class, stay in your small groups. Give each other feedback and discuss what you are learning from the role-playing. Then, we'll get ready for the last students' turns. When these are finished, we'll have a discussion to bring our thoughts together. Get ready. . . . (fade)

Another 7, this time for Crystal, but I don't think Jamie gets more than a 2. Crystal went first, and it was tough. As she said to us, in one of her frustrated moments, "Your behavior is not quite so perfect today, and it is very distracting!" In our group discussion, she admitted being completely disoriented. It was not what she had expected at all. It was hard, she said, gathering herself up to make the lesson work. I have to give her a lot of credit though. The lesson wasn't to-tally successful, by any means, but neither did she abandon it altogether. She really hung in. She too felt it wasn't a total loss and, all in all, thought the role-playing was good for her. She feels she learned to keep things going in a reason-able direction, even with a dozen distractions. Well, actually only four distrac-tions, but we were pretty big ones.

We must have gotten warmed up to the role-playing because Jamie got it from us even worse. I felt sorry for her. Our group was a perfect picture of the most unruly, obnoxious children you have ever seen. At first, there was a low murmur of talking. We simply ignored her. Steve T. said that he didn't understand the assignment. I began writing notes and giving them to my neighbors. Steve M. was cracking dumb jokes. Tiffany just sat there and stared out the window, like Totto-chan might have done. Jamie was trying to lead a discussion, but nobody would pay attention. Then, suddenly, a fight broke out and everyone except Tif-fany was hitting each other. At that point, Jerry came over and whispered in Jamie's ear. Afterward, she told us that he suggested that she stand up, move around, and discipline students face to face. It didn't help. Nothing she did was of any use, and finally she said, "End," before time was up.

We're waiting now for Jerry to call time. Watching the other groups, you can see misbehavior going on in every situation. It looks, though, like our group was the worst. I'm not sure what we are learning from this. At the moment, we're trying to console Jamie. . . . (fade)

(I don't encourage the widespread chaos that I'm witnessing. In fact, I discour-age it by regularly reminding students that successful role-playing requires a flex-ible balance of pressures. From experience, though, I have found that nothing I say seems to make a difference. Playing the role of difficult students always un-leashes the worst they can imagine. I have tried requiring half of the group to play positive roles, but the result is hardly any different. So I decided to instruct them to do what they are going to do anyway.

Sometimes I think the energy for mischief is archetypal—located deep in our psyches waiting for a chance to be released. Important learning does comes out of this chaos, but I'm sure even more would be learned if the role-playing were subtler. The transition from the earlier role-playing to the next rounds would be smoother too. I wonder if I could limit misbehavior to one student—insisting that all the other roles support the teacher.)

As you see, it's gotten quite chaotic in every group. Some of you may even be feeling seriously disappointed with yourselves as teachers. Postpone your worries for a few minutes. Before we get into a discussion about what can be learned from these experiences—besides a lot about frustration—I want to add the fifth and sixth round.

These will be more difficult because now I ask you to teach your group in front of the rest of the class. Everyone else will become the audience watching what happens. What we need are a couple of volunteers who believe they can do some things a little differently. Who imagines you could teach your lesson while coping with these uncooperative students? Anyone up for it? . . . Henry. . . . Don. Great, who wants to go first? . . . Henry. Good, set up your class and say, "Begin," whenever your are ready. . . . (fade)

It's me, Shaari, looking back on Henry's teaching at the end of the semester. I remember this class more vividly than any other. Everyone settled into their seats while he and his students got ready. "Begin," he said.

For his opener, he invited some general reactions to *Totto-chan*. There weren't two comments before, predictably, one of the students talked out of turn. Suddenly, Henry's face seemed to change. He was another person. He was yelling, practically screaming, "NO ONE TALKS UNLESS I CALL ON YOU, UNDERSTAND?" The students were shocked and tried not to laugh. Henry attempted to move on with the lesson. The students immediately started misbehaving again. He repeated his yell, "NO ONE TALKS UNLESS I CALL ON YOU." The students could not control their laughter.

He paused and quietly walked over to the door. The audience was looking back and forth between Henry and the students, and the students were momentarily stunned into silence watching to see what he would do next. I thought he was leaving the room, but no, he went to the light switch and flicked the lights on and off several times. He walked back to his students and sternly asked them if they were ready to behave. The students were trying to suppress their giggles. They couldn't, and neither could the audience.

I wondered if what was going through my mind was the same for anyone else. I was transported back to my high school days. For me, it was often just plain hell. Teachers like Henry were always yelling, and the response from the students was never positive. I responded to my high school teachers by drifting off to never-never land. One raised word toward me, and my eyes glazed. Teachers may have thought that I was hearing them, but in reality they were only yelling at a shell.

As I was observing "mean" Henry struggle, though, something else came to mind. The high school memories faded, and I began thinking about Henry's feelings. In place of experiencing someone yelling at me, as a student, I became more concerned for Henry, the teacher. I realized that he wasn't trying to be mean. He was only trying to competently do his job. What he wanted was his students to pay attention to him.

For a moment, I couldn't believe that I was on the teacher's side. Struggling along with Henry bumped up against how I used to behave. I felt dizzy. I also felt scared. We were only role-playing, and yet it was very real. I've been in classes where students have acted as badly as this, maybe worse. Big questions struck me: How would I act if not one student cooperated with me? How would I regain control of the class and get my students to take me seriously?

Well, the role-playing exercise is long since over, and poor Henry is off the hook. But I can still sense the frustration that he must have experienced. For me, it's feelings of helplessness and hopelessness. I have many ideas about the kind of teacher I want to be, but I'm a very easygoing person. And I am afraid that this could be my downfall. I worry that my students might walk all over me. Yet trying to be strict like Henry isn't helpful either. His way is a sure way to lose my students' interest and respect.

When I finally finish the teacher education program—I hope to graduate next year—I know my day will come. If I find myself in Henry's situation, at least now I'll know how not to act. I guess the best thing for me is to remember both my feelings for Henry and how I felt as a student. Maybe somewhere in between, I'll find a comfortable balance of friendliness and discipline. . . . (fade)

(How Henry played his role surprised even me. No matter how much I encourage creativity, sometimes students revert back to old familiar patterns they've experienced. Henry needs to be supported for his willingness to try out his views, and it's necessary to recognize that this must be where he is starting from. I want him to feel all right with trying out an alternative that didn't work. In class, role-playing is meant to be a safe place to do this. Also, without a corner on the truth, I don't want to say to him that his approach is wrong. Equally, though, I don't want to leave the impression that it is useful—in my eyes. I'm depending on the final discussion to provide some clarity.)

Henry, you are a true trooper. In our class discussion, we'll need to figure out together how you might have been more successful with these students. We'll also need to recognize the possibility that the roles the students played against you were probably too tough for anyone to handle.

Please think about three questions I want answered. One, even when a teacher is not successful, what strengths did you see? We will take time to point these out. Two, what could the teachers have done differently? We'll wonder together about what other approaches might have been helpful. And three—the question I'm most interested in—what personal needs did your misbehaviors express? From this inner knowledge, try to figure out what your teacher might have done to meet these needs and change your behavior during the role-playing. While Don takes his turn, keep these three questions in mind as a focus for our final discussion.

Not everyone will get a turn to role-play the teacher. If you are disappointed, rest assured that there will be other similar opportunities coming up this semester. Any questions before Don begins? . . . Shaari?

I have a couple of comments, not a question.

Go ahead.

I know that these role-playing situations are good because they show us some of the difficult problems we might face in the future. By comparison, though, they make me feel that the work I'm doing in my field placement is easy—right now. Helping out in a classroom by teaching small groups of children is mostly fun. I didn't realize how easy it was for me until I saw the role-playing. I also want to say—this is my last comment—I'm not disappointed. I feel lucky that I didn't have to role-play the teacher in my group.

6

Human Dominoes

Cast/Roll (in order of appearance)

One Year Ago

Shawn Poole:	Author, narrator, student, and starting member of group 3
Jerry Allender:	Author, director, teacher
Reneé and Hope:	Starting members of the two other groups
Andre:	2nd member
Dawn:	3rd member
Nary:	4th member
Anthony:	5th member
Kim:	6th member

Present Time

Tracy Heal:	Author, narrator, student, and Domino 1
Michele:	Domino 2
Steve T.:	Domino 3
Meredith:	Domino 4
Don:	Domino 5
Lauretta:	Domino 6
John:	Domino 7

There are three scenes. In the first, Shawn tells about a week one year ago describing the same lesson that is being taught this semester. The second scene is a retelling by the teacher of the first half of the same lesson today. Tracey's story, the third scene, recounts how the lesson ends this time.

❧

My name is Shawn Poole. I was in this course last year, and, for me, this week is easily remembered. It was my most difficult week of the term. It was when I joined a special group, and joining required a big risk that sort of fell on me. I call the story "Risky Business."

Like many of Jerry's students, even though I'm older than most, this was my first education course. By this point in the semester, I already knew that I liked the class. It particularly met my needs because it emphasized both the analytical and the creative sides of learning. It helped that Jerry encouraged us to use his first name. He was a professor you could talk with easily. Sometimes, teachers think students are only lumps of clay to be molded. Here, we were treated as real people. Given this background, on this day in class, my good mood was understandable. Our game of Human Dominoes was almost over.

We had a good time pretending we were dominoes. The funny little jokes lightened but didn't detract from what students thoughtfully said about their strengths and the skills they wanted to improve. Everyone seemed to take the game seriously. It was interesting to hear what we had to say about ourselves. It was helpful to find out more about our similarities—for strengths as well as weaknesses. By the end, the whole class was standing in a large twisted knot, everyone holding hands with three or four people, sometimes more, laughing, and waiting to be told what we were supposed to do now.

We were relieved, and laughed again, when he told us that we didn't have to hold each others' sweaty palms anymore. "Don't move though," he said. He wanted us to stay standing in the web while he discussed the purpose of the game. "An important goal of this activity is to learn how we have strengths and weaknesses in common. A deeper understanding of these feelings moves us closer to a conscious development of our teacher selves. We will continue to work on this development in various ways throughout the semester.

"I also asked you to play the domino game because it reveals interesting connections between people in class. Today, we are going to form new small groups for working on your own, from here on, for about an hour every week. From your experiences with previous partners, from other ways you've gotten to know students in this class, and from your connections at this moment in the web, think about who you would like to have in your group.

"Your big project, with a partner or two, will be to take turns team teaching a lesson to this new group. The taking of turns is similar to how each of you was the teacher in your small group last week, but this time you won't be role-playing. I'm going to help you plan a real part of our regular lessons. Your students, instead of confronting you with misbehavior, will act as good as they normally can—maybe even better. I want every one of you to have a chance to learn about your teaching abilities, in a relatively realistic situation, under the best possible conditions."

Jerry explained his method for choosing groups that would maximize our choices. We were going to divide our class of twenty into three groups. To begin, he asked for three volunteers to be the first person in each group—without knowing yet who would be in it. These are people, considering their experiences so far, who feel they would be comfortable working with anyone in class. He then asked for three more volunteers who were willing to postpone their choice to last. At that point, they would know everyone who was in each group, and they might get their favorite choice. But they also had to accept the possibility of joining any of the other groups because, finally, there would only be three choices left.

Jerry paused, and I wavered. I was willing to work with anyone in class, but I was cautious of finding out who wouldn't prefer to be in my group. What the heck, I thought. After all, our readings and our discussions since the beginning of the semester have pointed to a teacher's need for experimentation and risk taking. Now would be a good time to start. Besides, even if I'm not the most popular person in class, I am certainly not hated by anyone. Am I? Of course not.

Several people, including me, raised our hands, and Reneé, Hope, and I were chosen. Reneé and Hope became the first members of groups 1 and 2, and I was automatically put in group number 3. After that, three volunteers were picked for last choice.

From the remaining students, one person at a time was invited to join each of the three groups, in rounds. When the group you wanted came up, you were to raise your hand. Jerry was going to select one student for each of the three groups and then start the process over again—until everybody in class had joined a group. Because the opportunity for getting into a group would come up repeatedly, once every round, most students were likely to get their first choice. Because there wasn't any guarantee, though, Jerry asked us to be a little flexible. When we got to the end, those who agreed to go last would get to choose—or negotiate if there was a conflict.

In the first round, lots of hands immediately went up for group 1 and group 2. The process looked easy, and it was now my turn. Not one hand raised. There was a loud silence. Jerry didn't flinch. He took his time looking around for a few moments and finally said, "For this way of choosing groups, we have to wait until someone figures out that it would work for him or her to be in this group. If there isn't someone, we'll have to use another method."

Later, I would reason that most students probably wanted to join groups with people whom they already knew. Maybe they were in another class together, in the same dorm, or even roommates. Maybe they socialized together outside of class. Although I knew everyone's name soon after the semester started, people were still new to me. I lived off campus, and I had a full-time job that didn't leave much room for socializing. It's natural to be wary of joining a group with someone you don't know every well. I'd also been out sick recently for a few classes, so maybe people were just worried that I wouldn't be around when they needed me.

On that day though, waiting for what seemed to be a very long time, I felt like I didn't have a friend in the world. I fretfully wondered, Why don't people want to be in my group? Maybe it's because I express my opinions in class too often. I have been called arrogant before, but that was years ago. Besides, I think I'm willing to take criticism as much as I dish it out. Wait! I know. It's because I'm older than most of the other students. Those ageists! I mean, it's not like I'm Methuselah, for God's sake.

It was right at that moment that Andre moved from his place in the web and came to my side. I was so glad that someone had joined my group—to actually make it a group in more than name only. At least now, I thought, I'm not standing here alone. The sweet became a little bitter when I remembered that Andre had been one of the volunteers whose choice should have come last. Jerry quietly looked pleased and didn't say anything about Andre going out of turn. We moved on.

In the rounds that followed, Dawn, then Nary, then Anthony, and finally Kim joined us. As the group increased in size, I was feeling less and less awkward, but I knew I was still bruised. I couldn't resist thinking that these people really chose this group because they didn't care which group they were in. I decided they probably were all weird too. Andre is definitely weird, I was sure. He's always so quiet. And when he does talk, he usually cracks a joke. Does this guy really expect to be a good teacher? I don't know about this group, I said to myself.

In time, I would see the error of my first opinions. Andre and I wound up becoming partners for the team teaching project. I worked with him most closely, and it didn't take long for me to be convinced that he is going to be a great teacher someday. I saw in him, and much the same in the others, qualities that I think make for all great teachers: patience, creativity, understanding, humor, dedication, honesty, respect, discipline, flexibility, an interest in listening to others, and more.

Eventually, I felt honored to belong to this group—although not on that day. As the class drew to a close, I still felt so rejected. I got over it as I became more connected with the people in my group and the class. I even got to where I could laugh about that day. I risked, and I found myself in a terrific group.

Right after I tell my students that we are going to play a game called Human Dominoes, I always pause. . . . I wait a few seconds for some image to come to mind, and then I say, "No, I'm not going to line you up and push the first person in the line so that you all fall down on top of each other one after the next." I love the predictability of their laughter.

They will laugh like this in about fifteen minutes. The idea of standing in a line is already in their minds because I started class by dividing everyone into two rows, in the middle of the room, facing each other. I say, "You'll need a partner today for our beginning activity. If there is someone you want, be sure he or she is in the other line." I tell them it helps to put half of their small work group from last week on each side.

Now I have a whole class of undergraduate college students waiting and giggling like grade school kids. It's no different either. They're ready for something new, there is a looseness, yet I haven't lost control. "People in the line closest to me, turn around so that your backs face the students across from you. Those of you who are now in the line behind, walk over and pick a partner. It's not for sure you'll get who you want, but this way of choosing increases your chances. Remember, this is not a lifelong decision."

The activity is simple. All they have to do is sit down with a partner and share some of the strengths and weaknesses they believe about themselves as teachers. My instruction was, rather than to focus on weakness, to identify skills they want to improve and those for which they have some natural talent. I didn't set a time limit. It doesn't matter. They'll be ready for a change of pace soon enough. . . . (fade)

(I recently realized that I wasn't satisfied with how I teach this part of the course. Two students' stories in particular jarred my thinking. It took a long walk in the woods to sort through the threads of this dilemma. What is it, I thought, that is bothering me about my teaching this week? How could I teach differently? One of my goals at this point is to form small groups for the rest of the semester. Up till now, partners have only had to stay with each other for a week or two at the most. Even if it's not the best situation, students know they'll be out of it soon enough. Permanent groups need to be considered more carefully. It's a big deal whom one gets to work with, and I want my students to understand, for when they teach, some of the process involved in creating groups.

The way I have gone about forming groups has been developed over many years. It's important to me that students' choices are maximized, and I want them to have shared interests. I get used to old methods, and the "small" problems that come up from time to time often don't seem too important then. It disturbs me now that I discounted Shawn's moment of humiliation. To better understand how I might change this lesson, I took a closer look at my teaching by writing my version of class.)

Time's up. Now we're going to play Human Dominoes. The rules are easy. Everyone come stand in a large circle. . . . Remember, as a child, when you played dominoes. The tiles have two numbers on them, one on each end. One tile is joined with another by matching the numbers. Also, you are permitted to match a third tile, and even a fourth, at any union, to form branches. The result is a web of interconnected chains. That's it.

Each of you is a domino. Instead of numbers, you have strengths, on the one hand, and skills to improve, on the other hand. Literally. I need a volunteer who is willing to be our first tile. All you have to do is come into the middle of the circle, put one hand out, and tell us one of your strengths. Then, put your other

hand out and tell us one skill you'd like to improve. Who is willing? . . . Tracy
H. Come into the circle.

This seems a little silly.

Trust me. It'll get clear why we're doing this.

. . . Does it matter which hand I start with?

Nope.

Okay. On this hand, I think I'm intelligent and know a lot that I'll be able to
teach my students. On this hand, I'm worried that I won't be able to keep control
because I tend to be too easy with children. I don't want them to see me as mean.

Well done, but come back here. I need you to stay in the circle. Who will be
next? Who has a strength or an improvement that seems similar to either of
Tracy's hands? . . . Michele.

I'm sure I'm going to have difficulty keeping control because I tend to be quiet.
I hardly ever raise my voice, and I wonder if I need practice.

Which hand is that?

I'll make it my right.

Okay then, match it with Tracy's and hold hands. Now tell us about one of
your strengths.

I have a very open mind. I see myself learning as much from the children as
they learn from me.

Who's next? . . . Steve T.

On this hand, I already have many ideas about what I want to teach children.
Does that connect with Tracy's strength of belief in how much she knows?

Sure.

And on this hand, sometimes I might try to be too strict. I think my weakness
is the opposite of Tracy and Michelle. Do I have to hold Tracy's hand?

Yup. Come over here and take her free hand.

Meredith? You look like you're ready to be a domino.

I feel that I'm very flexible, and this would tie in with Michele's openness.
That's always been one of my strengths.

Great. Take Michele's hand. And on the other hand?

I'm not a good planner. Sometimes, I don't feel creative enough. I'd like to
improve my planning skills.

Don, you look like you're next.

I connect with both Meredith's weakness and her strength. I don't feel that
I'm a particularly creative person, but I'm a friendly easygoing guy. I find that
children naturally pay attention to me. Where do I go? Can I hold both of Meredith's hands?

Just one per customer. Let's have your easygoing friendliness form a branch
with Michele's and Meredith's openness and flexibility. We'll have two open
ends for wanting to improve creativity.

Remember, anyone can join anywhere on the line. Lauretta?

Well, I'm generally a pretty quiet person, but I don't know if this has to do with a skill I want to improve. Maybe because I'm a little older than Tracy and Michelle, I don't see myself backing down too easily. I expect children to pay attention to me, and, like Don, I find that they usually do. Still, I don't think being so quiet is a good model for my students.

What we're doing here isn't strictly dominoes. We don't have to follow the rules. Take Tracy's and Michele's hands, and we'll have a branch for quietness—knowing that the results won't always be the same. What's a for sure strength?

I'm very thorough. I'm big on being prepared. There will always be more than enough for my students to do.

John?

Maybe I'm similar to Lauretta. I could be the fourth branch for quietness. I could also take Lauretta's other hand for good planning, though I sometimes find it hard to decide what to do.

Either one is fine. You decide. . . . (fade)

Tracy H., that's how I'm called in class because there are two Tracys. In an earlier story, Tracy B. is the one who worried whether children in tough schools can be respectful students. That's not me, I'm Tracy Heal—with a different concern. Toward the end of the semester, to help us with our writing, Jerry gave us Shawn's story to read. I was bowled over. If I had been his classmate, I would have rejected him for sure. I seemed to be having the same experience as Shawn from the other side.

Like Shawn, I was one of the students who agreed to be put first in a group. There wasn't any problem, in my case, with getting people to choose the group, and I ended up with Lauretta, Don, Michele, Steve T., and John. At that point, there were just the six of us. I tend to be particular about the people I work with and had volunteered to be first with the misunderstanding that I would be choosing the members of my group. There were some students in the class that I had hoped to work with, and, to my dismay, with the exception of Lauretta, these did not include any of them.

Well, I thought, I would just have to deal with it. Our class was broken up into four groups, and Jerry asked us to begin by discussing the assignment. We needed to pick a partner for team teaching a lesson to our group. The lessons would be based on the three books we would be reading over the next six weeks. Our job was to subdivide into three teaching teams and choose the book each team wanted. I knew I wanted to use *The Education of Little Tree* as the basis of my lesson, and I asked the group if that was okay. It was fine with them. Good. Now I knew that I wanted to work with Lauretta, so I asked her if she knew what she wanted to do.

"I'm not quite sure," she replied.

I'm sure I can convince her, I thought. "It's a very interesting book. I'm sure you'll like it."

"I'd like to teach that book," John interjected.

Oh no! Not John! At the beginning of class today, I told Lauretta, who had picked me to do the activity in which we talked about some of our strengths and skills to improve, how hard it is for me to stand certain types of people. One type is someone who talks too much. That's why I think I would have rejected Shawn at first like everyone else. Another type is someone who is wishy-washy. To me, John was the epitome of this type. I knew I would have to face this problem if I got students with traits I don't like, but what was I going to do now? I pretended I didn't hear him. I went back to work on Lauretta.

"I'll lend you my book, Lauretta, and then you won't have to buy it," I offered selfishly.

"Thanks," she answered, "but I think John would like to do that one, and that's fine with me." She was just too nice.

"Yeah, I do," said John. To my chagrin, for someone who has rarely made his mind up in other class discussions, he was right on top of this one. "I've started the book, and I really like it."

I was stuck, and there was nothing I could do unless I wanted to seem like a horrible ogre. I decided I would take complete charge of the project, and all would go well.

My luck started turning for the better when Jerry came over to our group for us to tell him who the partners were, which books we had chosen, and the dates each team would be teaching. Before he left to go to another group, he asked, "Since Meredith is absent today and missed the dominoes exercise, is there any team that wants to claim her? If you do, she'll have her group and her partners all set to go when she comes back to class."

I jumped at the opportunity. "We'll take her. You don't mind, do you John?"

Meredith wasn't one of the students in class whom I knew well, but I was sure she would be a more decisive and energetic partner than my present one. I called her that evening and asked if she felt okay joining John and me. She was glad I called and said it was fine with her. She had chosen a different book than us, *Spinning Inward*, but we thought that would be all right. Jerry had said it was possible to plan a lesson using a combination of two books, and we agreed to talk it over when we would meet in class on Wednesday, two days later. There was hope.

Meredith and I arrived before class a bit early and immediately started talking. We soon realized we had a lot in common. We were both still wondering whether we really wanted to be teachers. We worried about being able to control our classrooms. We liked how, in this class, we were learning to take a more flexible attitude toward disciplining children and laughed over our resistance to change. I was pleased she was an outgoing person, and I felt we could work well together.

I told her about the kind of people I disliked and the irony of having John for a partner. She didn't have the same weakness as I, but she did have similar feelings about his indecisiveness. She also admitted that planning was her weak area. With her support, I said, I was confident that I could come up with a good plan for the three of us. When John arrived, it was time for class to begin, so we stopped socializing.

The first activity of the day took my mind off worrying about the planning we would have to do together. On a chart-sized piece of newsprint, with the marking pens we had used before, Jerry asked us to draw a sideways H. We drew an H lying on its side, from one side of the newsprint to the other, to create a large space at the top and the bottom, and two boxes in the middle. In the top space, we summarized some of the concepts we had learned in class so far. For the left box, we had to think about what helped our learning, and for the right, what might have hindered us. The space at the bottom was for goals for the rest of the semester, as we now see them.

Filling out the chart was easy. I was the recorder, and it was fun at first getting us to decide which color we should use for different ideas. It actually made sense for a while. In the top space, for what we learned, red indicated the importance of believing that every child deserves a chance to be taught. The concept of giving and receiving feedback was also written in red. Green means growth, so we chose it for the need to find positive aspects of children's learning experiences and for the idea of helping students recognize both their strengths and their weaknesses. Then Steve was insistent that we should use purple for the imagery method that Jerry taught us for learning everyone's name by the end of the first week of class. I said I didn't understand that one, but Don backed him up, and I got out the purple marker. The last concept for the top space was not to have set expectations. We chuckled when Meredith noted that, because we had two reds and two greens, we should have another purple. I shrugged my shoulders and wrote the concept in purple.

When we started to fill in the two middle boxes, for what helped and hindered our learning, I told the group that there wouldn't be anymore discussion about which color to use. The decision would be up to me, and my intuition, because I agreed to be the recorder. Everyone laughed, and Lauretta reminded us that we had better get more serious or we wouldn't finish before Jerry said we were out of time.

When I looked over the colors I chose for the ideas on what helped, I was a little embarrassed. I wrote readings in red, role-playing and the domino game in green, feedback and observing each other teach in purple, and discussions in black. That the class discussions were a big help to our learning was John's idea. I hope nobody noticed that maybe I was expressing my mood about John. I decided that I had better stop paying attention to the colors.

We didn't have much to write down for what hindered our learning, but I thought the few ideas we got were important. Michele, who is very quiet, said she was uncomfortable when she had to become the center of attention in class. Lauretta and John chimed right in and said they had similar feelings. To that we all added that our fears and frustrations were a regularly occurring problem. We also all agreed that Jerry's expectations gave us a heavy workload inside and out-side of class.

By the time we got to figuring out our goals for the bottom of the chart, I think we were a little tired of the discussion. The goals we came up with were pretty general: to overcome fears, strengthen weaknesses, find successful ways to teach all different children, stay open-minded, have stamina, and learn how to always be patient, persistent, and encouraging. And, for a last one, Steve had us add—and, of course, Don pushed his idea—to reach our goals. I didn't think we were being realistic. To me, our set of goals looked more like a laundry list. Though, when Jerry came over to check on what we were doing, even though he didn't say anything, he seemed to be satisfied. . . . (fade)

(Jerry) If you are still adding goals in the bottom space of the newsprint, finish writing the one you are working on and then stop. . . . Form our usual large circle. . . . Look over the chart as a whole and think of it as a picture—in words—of yourselves as a group of students. When you take your turns team teaching the group, keep in mind what you have learned about your students' knowledge, attitudes, and goals. Now it's time to get together with your partners and start planning. Find your own little space to meet by spreading out all over the classroom. . . .

I want you to organize your planning around five resources: (1) the theme for the week's teaching that you can find in the syllabus, (2) the books you chose, (3) the teaching experiences you are having each week in your school, (4) a learning activity that will make your teaching interesting for your students, and (5) a sample lesson for children that you adapt for your adult students. This is a lot, and maybe you won't manage to include all that I am asking. Think of using these five resources as an ideal and see how close you can get. Keep in mind that you will have an hour to fill. Whatever you do, it is most important to plan a lesson with which *you* are comfortable. It has to be one in which all the parts and pieces fit together easily.

So, begin by imagining your ideal lesson and work to make it practical as you move along. I'll come around and answer questions and give suggestions when-ever you feel you need help. Even though our time left today is short, it should be enough for each team to clarify the assignment for itself. If not, we'll take more time next week, or, if you want, I'll make arrangements to meet with you before or after class. Once you understand what you need to do, schedule a meet-ing for your team outside of class to finish the planning. . . . (fade)

(Tracy) I came to the meeting with lots of ideas for what we could do—enough for me, Meredith, John, and others had there been more of us. At the outset, everything went well—one might say, according to my devious plan. Mer-edith's ideas and mine dovetailed easily. But then John wanted to do something different. In my biased mood, I didn't think his ideas were good enough, and I kept offering more of my own. He stuck by his guns. He thought he had a good plan and decided that's what he would do for his part. Why was he being so decisive now? There was nothing I could do to dissuade him. I could only hope that Jerry would be busy watching other groups and not be around much when it was our turn to teach.

D day arrived, and I was extremely nervous. We made a few last-minute changes, but we all felt prepared. Meredith was first. To open our theme about the emotional side of learning, she led a relaxation exercise that she had adapted from *Spinning Inward,* the book she had read. Everyone said they enjoyed it, but it took less time than we had planned.

Then it was my turn. I asked our students to role-play some of the problems they were having with the children they were teaching. What I wanted was for us to get an understanding of the children's feelings in each situation. For the most part, though, we kept taking the teacher's side. I thought the role-playing went well anyway because everyone got the point. However, it too didn't go quite as planned, and, again, the time it took was shorter than we had expected.

John's turn. We had more time left than we had planned for, and I was sure we would be embarrassed by running out of what to do before the time was over. Worry, worry, that's me. I fidgeted while he was getting his materials organized. Everyone else seemed relaxed enough, and when he began speaking, I couldn't believe it. He was an entirely different John!

He had read his book, *The Education of Little Tree,* twice, and he had prepared several thought-provoking questions. He told us he wasn't sure of his own answers to these questions and hoped the discussion would help to clarify his opinions. Saying that seemed to stimulate the discussion. He had command of the situation and everyone's attention! The question I liked best was, Why would teachers of a young Indian boy in a white school be so unsympathetic? We got to talking about how much more Little Tree had learned while he was living for a year with his grandparents way back in the hills and not going to school. John felt that many children's problems in school are created by the ways teachers treat them.

It was a good day. John led an energetic discussion, it connected all three parts of our lesson, and it wasn't even over at the end of the period. He filled up the rest of the time, and we could have gone on longer. I felt bad for doubting him. Sorry, John. . . . (fade)

It's been over a month now since I took a walk in the woods to think about this story. I've been busy writing—interweaving Shawn's and Tracy's stories with my own. I recognized that my way of forming groups to do independent work over the rest of the semester was not trouble free. I don't imagine that my students' learning can happen without difficulty, but I think it's my job, if I can figure out how, to make it easier. I was holding on too tightly to an assumption about maximizing students' choices. Often, it is important, but my experiences teaching children showed that just as often a teacher has an important role in choices as well. From the writing of this story, it's clear that adults are not essentially different in this regard.

When the assumption was amended, a new vision emerged. When all of the students are standing and holding hands at the end of the domino game, I'll ask them to figure out three or four obvious roughly equal-sized pods that make up the web. The goal is to have six to nine students in each. After deciding, I'll tell them that each pod will be a group for working together in the weeks to come. Without describing the whole project—without making a big deal—it will be easy for the students to do a couple of well-defined tasks. I'll have them draw a diagram of each of their hands and whom they were connected with in their pod to record their personal strengths and the skills they wanted to improve.

On a second piece of newsprint, they will create the group "picture" with spaces for concepts learned, what helped and hindered their learning, and goals. After a few minutes of this commotion, they'll stop and think about what their group picture looks like. In a small square in the middle of the newsprint, I'll ask them to put a word, or two, or three, or a symbol, that characterizes their group as a whole. By this time, it will be close to the end of Monday's class.

At the beginning of Wednesday's, each group will analyze its own diagram and picture. The groups will be instructed to use this information to break up the pod into subgroups of two or three. Given what we have been doing so far, it shouldn't be difficult to do. If the activity goes smoothly, the groups and the teams will now be in place without the previous stress.

I like the challenge of new plans. It's not possible to know how they'll succeed, but it excites me to know I'll find out. One way or the other, or in some middle ground, I'm sure to learn something new about the art and science of teaching. What perplexes me, though, is how to judge success. From John's journal, I discovered that he had a very different experience than Tracy. In his last journal entry, he wrote about working with Don, Steve, Meredith, Tracy, Lauretta, and Michelle: "This turned out to be the greatest group I've ever been involved with in school."

7

Midterm Paper

The Problem of Realness

> "What is REAL?" asked the Rabbit one day, when they were lying side by side near the nursery fender, before Nana came to tidy the room. "Does it mean having things that buzz inside you and a stick-out handle?"
>
> "Real isn't how you are made," said the Skin Horse. "It's a thing that happens to you. When a child loves you for a long, long time, not just to play with, but REALLY loves you, then you become Real."
>
> —From *The Velveteen Rabbit* by Margery Williams

Like the Rabbit, I as a teacher started out not knowing the answer to the problem of realness, not even that I had one. It might be too that the problem is solved by love, but when I think about teaching, the process is clearly more complex (not to say that it wasn't complex for the Rabbit as well). Right after Rabbit establishes how he might become real, he has the sense to ask, "Does it hurt?" and the Skin Horse answers, "Sometimes," for he was truthful. Rabbit's questions are relevant for teachers, no less for students, and they are a useful place to begin.

I begin with the assumption that the primary source of knowledge for developing oneself as a teacher is personal. I don't discount or demean other kinds of knowledge—that which is derived from scholarly investigations or distilled and demonstrated from long experience—it is just that they have a lower priority in my scheme of thinking. The essence of teaching, and, therefore, the essence of learning how to teach, is in the development of one's teacher self. This is how a teacher becomes real.

For reasons that certainly have to do with difficult childhood experiences in school, my greatest concerns in teaching center around accessing intuitive knowledge, vitality, and spontaneity. Growing up, I didn't lack for intellectual stimulation, or even opportunities to be creative, but these other qualities of experience were strongly de-emphasized, particularly in connection with learning. I felt that something important was missing, and I yearned (mostly unconsciously, but clearly now) for connections between my intellectual growth and the other parts of my rich inner life. I have found that by focusing on the development of my teacher self I can access the inner knowledge that is needed to be a successful teacher. And with this approach, I continue to discover that it is possible to help students tap these strengths in themselves.

There are dangers, of course. Teaching that ignores the value of intellectual and experiential knowledge will be no less incomplete than a curriculum that discourages self-development. This has been a constant concern of mine over years of teaching, and it has always been a question of balance—which regularly needs attention and adjustments. Equally persistent, however, and where one is most liable to hurt, is the discomfort of vulnerability. Tapping inner strengths is not possible without an openness to vulnerability. It is all too easy to hide behind the wealth of knowledge and interesting teaching techniques that an experienced teacher develops. Entertaining and informative lectures and demonstrations, questions and answers, and many kinds of group activities can fill up classroom time. But to fully help students develop a real teacher self, as we learn from the Skin Horse, requires something more.

I don't believe, though, that vulnerability is a fair demand in just any learning environment. It requires one that fosters highly interactive relationships with students and conditions that encourage similarly interactive relationships among the students themselves. For me, this approach is based on the writings about humanistic education. A central concept is the priority given to people over ideas. First come the needs of the students who are being taught, and second are the readings, concepts, and skills that the teacher feels need to be covered.

Neill's *Summerhill*, clearly expressing the social and political climate of the 1960s, pictures this priority in an extreme form.[1] When I began teaching, the book had a pervasive influence on my thinking. I was captured by the school Neill describes—with as much freedom for children's learning as anyone could imagine. The development of relationships between teachers and students was the predominant activity, and sometimes, indeed, it was the only one.

The practicality of using Summerhill as a model for my teaching soon came to an end. A student, whom I had only seen once before, on the first day of class, showed up to ask a question at the beginning of the fifth week. Something I said communicated that it was unnecessary for students to come to class. This was consistent with a tendency to believe that Neill's philosophy means that students are permitted to do anything they want. Subsequently, asking my students to notice the underlying interpersonal dynamics that facilitate how Summerhill functions successfully day to day helped *me* become more sensitive to the kind of structure that a teacher needs to provide. It was obvious that a relationship isn't possible with a student who never attends!

Three Rogerian concepts being developed around this same time, and still current in the most recent edition of *Freedom to Learn* (as well as fundamental for probably every variation of psychotherapy that is practiced today), proved to be insightful: acceptance, empathy, and realness.[2] For teaching, acceptance meant finding ways to regularly let students know what is valuable about their learning. I had to shift the balance of criticism and praise far in the direction of telling students how they are succeeding. Empathy meant that I must be aware of my student self in an effort to understand, in great depth, students' experiences of learning. These two concepts supported what I was trying to accomplish as a teacher.

Sufficiently understanding the concept of realness was more difficult. In order to express acceptance and to be as empathetic as possible, I was choosing not to express frank opinions that I imagined would get in the way of students' learning. The initial solution was the application of Maslow's theory about the value of providing conditions of learning that ensure a student's sense of safety being slightly greater than the pressures that stimulate growth.[3] He argues that the need for safety is stronger than the need for growth. Potential learning is most enhanced when students can respond to challenges without worrying about the consequences of their mistakes. Teaching with this in mind, I found room for a fuller expression of what I wanted from my students and what I felt and thought about their work.

The goal of my teaching gradually transformed into setting up challenges that strengthened, not threatened, students' positive feelings about their learning. Against the background of more acceptable traditional methods of teaching, my efforts were seen by colleagues as progressive and often too radical. Just as there has been a shift, though, with the application of Rogers's ideas, over time, I eventually found this aspect of my teaching nearer to center stage. Support came additionally from Noddings's arguments for a much larger role of caring in schools.[4] She clarifies the need for making students feel safe in an adventure of significant, challenging learning.

No matter; daily, there are always classroom problems to face—for teachers of any philosophical predisposition. In *Growing Minds,* Kohl describes different facets of the relationships that exist between teachers and students, and a reoccurring theme is the ways in which students resist learning.[5] The stories he tells broaden the perspective for what *a teacher might do* when *students don't do* what is asked of them. There are many creative, humanistic examples. Though only some lead to successful outcomes, his stories overall sensitized me to watch for what my students really need so that I can respond more creatively.

A larger framework for addressing resistance came to me from stories by Kuroyanagi, in her book *Totto-chan,* about a progressive school in Japan that she attended in the 1930s.[6] Its similarity to Summerhill was brought home to me when some of my students said that *Totto-chan* describes a school where children can do anything they want. This school too provided a wider range of choice and greater degrees of freedom than one is likely to actually find—in any country. In contrast to images of resistance, however, it is the headmaster's focus on children, nature, culture, music, adventure, and most of all listening that these stories highlight. More than anything else, this focus conveys excitement. It is translated into a learning environment that effectively sets boundaries and yet supports, and encourages, a true sense of freedom in the classroom.

The goals of this school are achieved with a minimum of direction and control. There is apparently less need for student resistance, which usually takes up so much of our attention as teachers. The headmaster succeeds at making his students feel both safe and challenged through a mixture of trust and vulnerable, personal contact—in Rogers's terms, acceptance and realness. It is the latter, his willingness to personally engage with his students, not the content and cleverness of his lessons, that most importantly connects him with his students.

Yet, in spite of similar concerns for personal engagement, I usually find myself trying to improve the practice of teaching based on reactions to student resistance. How I change my teaching strategies is a response most of all to learning activities and interactions with students that aren't working smoothly. This is a far cry from the images of excitement conveyed in *Totto-chan* that are so attractive. These images encourage me to think about strengths, interests, uniqueness, and wonder and about finding ways to keep them in the forefront. They relate to the excitement that is the core of the intuitive knowledge, vitality, and spontaneity toward which I aim. *Totto-chan* reveals how these aims are not only goals but also a path toward their development.

Because defensiveness is such a natural response, teachers tend to react dysfunctionally to students' resistance. Helpfully, Kuroyanagi recognizes that there is an interplay between resistance and excitement. The difficulties that resistance poses can be reframed more productively as a conflict between the teacher's excitement and the students' excitement. In a compelling example, the headmaster practices a verbal aikido with a first grader's resistance to school (Kuroyanagi, when she was a child) by turning it into a fascinating welcoming conversation. It lasts all morning, with the student doing most of the talking, just between the two of them. In this conversation, there had to be numerous moments of difficulty for both the student and the teacher. But the teacher's respect and the student's respect in response overcame these moments.

Recent reading suggests how a better match of the teacher's and students' excitement is achieved. Cohler and Galatzer-Levy, in an article on psychoanalysis and the classroom, point to the importance of looking at the relationship between the teacher and the student as a potential interactional space, where both contribute to the construction of its meaning.[7] In the 1970s, I explored the development of common meaning for building mutual trust in open classrooms, but that conception favored the role of the student and proved unworkable.[8] Today, the teacher's responsibility for guiding students is paramount.

It is the teacher's job, on the one hand, to protect students from experience that is too difficult for them and, on the other hand, to stand back while they are confronted with realistic difficulties. But students can want and not want to be protected all at once. The significance of a cartoon in the days of the open classrooms—in which a young child says to the teacher, "Do we have to do what we want to do?"—rings true. It is normal for students both to want guidance and to complain and resist whatever is required.

Winnicott, discussing this kind of interactional space and its relevance to child rearing, points out in a talk directed at parents that all the while that they are maintaining boundaries for their children, they are to expect defiance.[9] He advises that resistance to boundaries is desirable because it is indicative of a child's healthy growth and that, while disciplining children, parents also need to gradually let the world in. Escalating conflicts, the sense of difference, is what doesn't work. Working creatively with the resistance does. In the context of a satisfying relationship, the experience of security that parents provide their children leads to an interest in self-regulation and internal feelings of being safe enough to venture out.

I think similar principles apply to classroom teaching. When a student receives this kind of flexible, responsive guidance, independent behaviors naturally increase. Self-direction, without an interactive relationship, in contrast, is expectantly the occasion for mismatched desires between teacher and student. What can reverse this expectation are teachers' awareness of the complexity of their role and a sensitivity to students' complex needs. Over time, a history of a mutually gratifying relationship can be built that makes it possible to foster responsible independence. The interplay that joins teacher and student is necessarily dynamic.

An obstacle to creating this kind of dynamic learning environment is the gatekeeper role of the teacher. Too much energy is spent on judging the quality of students' learning, grading, and telling them how they are wrong. The gatekeeper job interferes with the intention to support students sufficiently so that they may venture out on their own. Cohler and Galatzer-Levy say that, in addition to self-reliance, it is equally important for students to learn how to use others as a source of affirmation and comfort, throughout life. It is odd that there is a high expectation in our culture for parents to soothe children's stress—and therapists, their clients—but much less so for teachers. Besides protection from harm, this is the important avenue for making continued learning of any kind feel attractive and possible in the face of one's fears. Even successful teachers need to know how to act as just such an ally.

The role of ally is better suited to the interactive relationship that I want with my students. For sure, I know I don't improve in this role by simply favoring the desires of students, nor do I want to act as a parent, therapist, or close friend. One image, involving the balance of safety and challenge, is stimulated by Bernstein's argument that self-esteem is best catalyzed by giving students the courage to try.[10] In terms of his psychoanalytic interpretation, how others feel about us is not the salient factor that affects our sense of competence. The important source of self-esteem is the accumulation of the experience of successfully accomplishing what we set out to do—and without it, we will not be convinced.

Self-evaluation is the significant factor, and a teacher can only assist by providing opportunities for successful experience. This image fits with the concept of the teacher as an ally, who supports the courage to try, with a stronger emphasis on the *limits* of positive and negative feedback, however constructive.

I am also drawn to another image of an ally, the enlightened witness about which Alice Miller writes.[11] This refers to the special support that someone can give others, in answer to their inner conflicts, toward awareness and clarity of thought and feeling. If a teacher were careful not to be a therapist, maybe some of these conflicts too could be addressed in the classroom. But it is more how one acts as this witness that attracts me as a teacher. An ally of any kind is meant to give someone the courage to try. But the enlightened witness is concerned with the courage of awareness and connection, not achievement. I see in this ways of paying attention to students and encouraging the expression of feelings that might shift the focus from resistance to a focus on their needs. Of essence, the teacher must not be judgmental. There has to be enough time to fully hear what the student has to say. The intention, in the teacher's response, is to convey to the student that he or she is worthy of regard. The student is a valuable person who deserves to be heard.

I worry that listening so carefully to one student can be problematic, particularly when a teacher and a student disagree. I know that when there is strong disagreement, and the interaction between a student and me is highlighted and prolonged, classmates are likely to react to the class time spent as an interruption and interference. Because I am a teacher and not a therapist, it is important that the overall class goals are not lost. There will be times when discussions need time outside of class to be completed, but for the development of an interactional space, everyone's involvement and support are far better.

Ideally, all conversation should be perceived as part of the ongoing flow of class activities. The only avenue I have found is to experiment. I want to understand the student from his or her point of view, to affirm the trustworthiness of our relationship, and to maintain appropriate boundaries. As we are growing together, I hope that new possibilities will emerge. Maybe I can change, then and there. Maybe the student will come to a different view. Given neither of these, maybe, at least, we (including others in the class) will achieve a better understanding of each other that serves to ease the conflict. My responsibility, still, whatever the outcome, is to give direction that helps us move on.

Another view of resistance is to see the student as a problem. One way out of fully engaging with students is to decide what is wrong with them, not the relationship, and then, at best, search for an approach that might alleviate the difficulties with which they struggle. Even therapists, whose job it is to diagnose psychological problems, run the risk of distancing themselves from clients by labeling them, thereby closing themselves off from each person's uniqueness. It is the same for teachers. In *Learning and Education: Psychoanalytic Perspectives*, edited by Field, Cohler, and Wool, there are many examples of dysfunctional learning that are intrinsically connected with the fuller context of students' lives out-side of the classroom.[12] To know and understand these difficulties, and ways to modify one's guidance with them in mind, is often relevant and helpful. How-ever, this view has drawbacks. Equally for educators and therapists, the potential of the interactional space for facilitating learning is more restricted than it would be otherwise.

The primary attention should be on the relationship between the teacher and the students. Interactions based primarily on label-bound behaviors of teachers and students, as with any labels, detract from unhampered interactions that are a part of engaging in a lively relationship. The problem is the same as typecasting behavior. It is simpler for teachers to interact with students within the confines of their respective traditional roles. As I point out earlier, classroom energy is spent most safely and comfortably communicating information and skills. We see now the danger of fulfilling this responsibility at the cost of contactful inter-action. A teacher's responsibility for maintaining boundaries and the curriculum cannot be ignored, yet risk taking is essential to realness. The dialectic between these two poles has to be reexamined regularly.

Without a delicate balance between enacting any role and more connected contact, the ability to establish a responsive relationship can be lost. Whether coping with classroom disagreements or aiming in general for exciting teaching and learning, there must be regular movement outside of normally expected in-teraction. In the office of a psychotherapist, Whitaker and Napier both demon-strate that the distance can go so far as to include antics that are outrageous and illogical.[13, 14] Their work embodies an underlying pervasive humor that, I think, releases the creative energy for generating sensible, however far-fetched, possibil-ities. For Whitaker, indeed, acting spontaneously—with its concomitant in-crease in self-disclosure and vulnerability—is the quintessence of being real.

The greatest potential for learning exists in an interpersonal environment that is real. Working at lowering resistance and raising excitement, the encoun-ter of unpredictable developments and outcomes of teaching and learning is a shared adventure in the classroom. Everyone benefits, the teacher and the stu-dents, as they learn from each other.

NOTES

1. Neill, A. S. 1960. *Summerhill: A radical approach to child rearing*. New York: Hart.

2. Rogers, C. R., and H. J. Freiberg. 1994. *Freedom to learn*, 3rd ed. New York: Merrill.

3. Maslow, A. H. 1968. *Toward a psychology of being*, 2nd ed. Princeton, N.J.: D. Van Nostrand.

4. Noddings, N. 1992. *The challenge to care in schools: An alternative approach to educa-tion*. New York: Teachers College Press.

5. Kohl, H. 1984. *Growing minds: On becoming a teacher*. New York: Harper & Row.

6. Kuroyanagi, T. 1982. *Totto-chan: The little girl at the window*. Trans. D. Britton. New York: Kodansha International.

7. Cohler, B. J., and R. M. Galatzer-Levy. 1992. Psychoanalysis and the classroom: Intent and meaning in learning and teaching. In *Educating the emotions: Bruno Bettelheim and psychoanalytic development*, ed. N. M. Szajnberg, pp. 41–90. New York: Plenum.

8. Allender, J. S. 1976. The role of the teacher in student-directed learning. In *Real learning: A sourcebook for teachers*, ed. M. L. Silberman, J. S. Allender, and J. M. Yanoff, pp. 301–06. Boston: Little, Brown.

9. Winnicott, D. W. 1993. *Talking to parents*. Reading, Mass.: Addison-Wesley.

10. Bernstein, H. E. 1989. The courage to try: Self-esteem and learning. In *Learning and education: Psychoanalytic perspectives*, ed. K. Field, B. J. Cohler, and G. Wool, pp. 143–57. Madison, Conn.: International Universities Press.

11. Miller, A. 1990. *Banished knowledge: Facing childhood injuries*. Trans. L. Vennewitz. New York: Doubleday.

12. Field, K., B. J. Cohler, and G. Wool, eds. 1989. *Learning and education: Psychoanalytic perspectives*. Madison, Conn.: International Universities Press.

13. Whitaker, C. 1989. *Midnight musings of a family therapist*. New York: W. W. Norton.

14. Napier, A. Y. 1978. *The family crucible*. New York: Harper Perennial.

8

Superteacher Meets Blue Orange

At this point in the semester, the students take over more responsibility for their own learning, including some of the teaching, and I no longer see myself as the director of a play. A list of characters isn't relevant; nor are the many stage directions and asides that have been regularly appearing in parentheses.

Pretend, instead, that you are a student in my class. The focus this week is on a new theme: the cognitive side of learning. By way of introduction, I'll illustrate the ease with which the mind can take in new information and the potential power that teachers have for helping students learn. From an imaginary story, you will learn a fact you will *never forget*.

So, prepare yourself. In saying this, chemical processes are activated in the brain to make a place for the information. Get ready, get set . . . your brain is waiting . . . here we go. There is an island I never heard of in the Pacific Ocean where orange trees grow blue oranges. Inside and out. **BLUE ORANGES.**

You will certainly forget some of these details. It is not unlikely that where you learned about blue oranges, from a book, its name and author, will be forgotten. Even that the story takes place in the Pacific Ocean, that it is a story told as an introduction to discussing the cognitive side of learning, whether it is imaginary or real, or anything else about the context. These are easily forgotten. But what will be remembered is the *possibility of blue oranges*. In class, I insure myself, and the students, of the truth of my prediction by then unveiling a large painting of a blue orange—filling up most of the canvas with the word *Sunkist* largely printed on the blue skin. Laughter cements the memory.

Discussing the experience with my students, a variety of reasons explain the apparent truth of this outlandish prediction. Because the information is so unusual is the most popular explanation. Another common explanation has to do with seeing a picture. Others include that it is one simple "fact," that the idea is connected with a story, that it is related to an intriguing fantasy, that multisensory learning is involved, or that the information has been transformed into a direct experience of learning. These are the kinds of concepts we are now reading about in the text *Teaching for the Two-Sided Mind* by Linda Williams, which is assigned for this theme. I can honestly say that I don't know the correct an-

75

swer, except that it is sure to be somewhat different for every person, depending on one's style of learning.

The story also creates the conditions for understanding what happens next. From each small group, I ask for two or three students to volunteer as a subteam for planning a one-hour lesson to teach the rest of their group. The task is to teach a multiplication table that is realistically difficult for adults—the squares of 12 to 25—using concepts from the text and others we are discussing on how learning is facilitated. When the task is assigned, I will challenge the subteams to help the other members of the group, who will be their students, to remember these squares as easily as a blue orange.

Note to the reader: There is a test at the end of the chapter. Please pay close attention to the math lesson.

(Since Jerry doesn't need these parentheses to be the director anymore, I'm going to use them. At the Media Elementary School, in the third-grade class one morning every week when I'm helping out Mrs. Smith, who is teaching my eldest son, I am Superteacher!

Well, at least, I *was* Superteacher. The kids might not see the difference, but this week I lost the secret power to change clothes in a nearby telephone booth and transform myself. I am stuck in my hidden identity, humble Bryant Chavous, student at Temple University, dual major in math and teacher education. Everyone in Jerry's class heard about what had happened. When Mieke and Nick, my group's teachers, asked their students, me included, to learn the squares of 12 to 25, I didn't pay attention because I'm a math major. Then came the test. I only got four of the answers right—while everyone else had close to a perfect score. Extra! Extra! Read all about it. Supermathteacher falls out of the sky and hits the pavement, hard.

Last week in Mrs. Smith's class, everything was still going fine, including *cucumber*. With third graders, any word can be a silly word, and this morning it was *cucumber*. Mrs. Smith again had asked me to take Benjamin, Greg, and Kenneth to one of the tables in the back of the room for help in arithmetic. Before getting started, the kids and I were talking for a minute about next week's spelling list. Maybe we shouldn't have sneaked a look at what was coming up, but I like having fun with them. Greg said, "Cucumber," then the other two said, "Cucumber?" and they laughed for nearly a minute. They were so delighted, I couldn't keep myself from smiling.

There was going to be an arithmetic test the following day, so I knew that we had to settle down and prepare. Kenneth was unfamiliar with my system for making a multiplication chart because he had been absent. To get us all to the same place, I reviewed the chart for everyone. It didn't take long for Benjamin to remember what I had showed him after slowly, just once, going over how the chart was made. He took a sheet of problems and was off and running. Greg, always looking for attention, needed a little coaxing. I lured him with my eyes and in-sisted, after reviewing the chart a second time, that he too knew how to do the problems. There were only a few questions from either of them while they were working on their own. When Benjamin and Greg were finished, I sent them back to their seats.

For Kenneth, it wasn't so easy. I didn't realize how difficult multiplication ta-bles can be for an eight year old. We worked together well past the end of the period. I feel that all any kid needs sometimes is a little extra time and some one-on-one help. Even so, it seems that Kenneth is going to need an awful lot of extra help and lots of practice. In addition to his difficulty catching on, I won-dered whether he was interested. His attention kept wandering every few minutes.

Before I was ready to quit, Mrs. Smith asked Kenneth to come back with the rest of the class. She was putting an outline on the blackboard and wanted every-one there to learn about book reports. I came along and sat down in one of the empty seats near the kids. I like listening to lessons as if I were just another stu-dent. Teaching third graders is new to me, and I thought I might get better at it by putting myself in Kenneth's place. I tried to imagine what he was thinking.

Though I didn't know it then, Jerry and I had similar concerns. This was the week he dismissed class a half hour early. Only the students who had volunteered to teach the small groups for this theme had to stay after. He said they had to attend a teachers' meeting. Later, we found out that this was when Mieke and Nick, and the other group teachers, were given the task of teaching us the squares of 12 to 25. But first they themselves had to learn them: one, because they were the teachers and, two, because Jerry wanted the teachers to understand their students better. He'll tell you about it himself.)

I insist that the teachers like Mieke and Nick, before preparing how to teach the lesson, first learn the squares themselves. This is my immediate concern. For starters, to entice them, I gamble that they will be intrigued to know that this task was invented for a third grader who had learned all his multiplication tables and had nothing to do while the others in the class were still struggling. Plus, it is useful to recognize that this multiplication table is easier than the others chil-dren normally learn because it only involves fourteen simple associations. Ordi-narily, for a multiplication table, one has to know the result of two different numbers multiplied times each other. Here though, for example, $12 \times 12 = 144$ is the same as *the square of 12 is 144*. There is just the relationship of two numbers to remember, 12 and 144.

I point out my basic motivations. Besides hoping that my students will find creative ways to facilitate learning while memorizing the multiplication table of these fourteen squares, I want them to work on developing empathy for their students. The assignment allows for clear movement back and forth between feeling and thinking like both a student and a teacher. All the students in class have the opportunity to imagine themselves as the children whom they are as-signed to tutor in local schools, while the students who have volunteered to teach can also focus on empathizing with their classmates who will soon be their students, facing this same task, early next week. Although this experience is primarily related to subjects for which memorization is required, it is a good place to begin learning about what is happening in a student's mind.

One suggestion I have for the subteam is to divvy up the squares among the teachers and organize the lesson in three parts. Of the fourteen squares, for most people, six are quite easy, and it's helpful if each part includes two of these. Notice that when all the numbers are reversed in $12 \times 12 = 144$, which people generally know, the result is $21 \times 21 = 441$. Once seen, this too is usually remembered—like a blue orange. These two easy squares are good ones for part 1.

Like any other multiplication table, others are of medium difficulty, and some doggedly resist staying in one's accessible memory. Similarly, these need to be divvied up. For example, 13×13 and 14×14 are of medium difficulty because their squares form a related pattern. Multiplying just 3×3 and 4×4 lets one know that the answers end in 9 and 6. Because the square of 13 is 169 and the square of 14 is 196, by thinking about them as a pair, there is enough information to deduce the answers almost instantly. The strain of remembering these squares is reduced because they are partial reversals of each other.

For the last square in part 1, I like $24 \times 24 = 576$. It is typically one of the more difficult squares, but I have found an association for remembering it that has stuck with me. I am reminded of the year of America's birthday, the big celebrations we had in 1976, all of the showy hoopla. Furthermore, since this is the next to the highest of the squares, I know it is one of the higher numbers in the table, a "five hundred something." In my mind, 5 - - is what I visualize, and immediately America's birthday fills in the two blank spaces. Without too much difficulty, I then know that the square of 24 is 576.

Now, for finishing up the first part of the lesson, I suggest a second visualization. In the mind's eye, put the squares of $12 = 144$ and $21 = 441$ and the squares of $13 = 169$ and $14 = 196$ inside a blue orange—symbolizing the circularity, that is, the reversing aspect of their relationships. And leave the square of $24 = 576$ outside of the blue orange as a symbol of its independence.

Given that only five squares are tackled so far, I'm not surprised when these associations work well for most people. The problem of remembering just five can be lightweight for many of us. The next challenge, in part 2, is to memorize five additional pairs from the multiplication table without feeling overloaded.

(Had I paid attention to this much of the lesson, I would have at least gotten five right. To begin with, I arrived late for class. Mieke was in the middle of showing us flash cards when I sat down in my seat—checking how much we already knew. I remember my reaction, "This is stupid!" I was annoyed with the idea of another student acting like my teacher. It's embarrassing to admit, but stemming from the image of myself as Superteacher, I felt that other students weren't up to my level of knowledge, skill, dedication, or desire for perfection. I justified my attitude by telling myself I was older, a parent, and living on my own since I was seventeen. My mind was closed, and instead of getting involved I whispered a side conversation with Alex about going fishing—pretending I was getting his help to catch up. He is easy to distract.

After the flash cards, Nick gave a short introductory lecture. He summarized the main concepts in *Teaching for the Two-Sided Mind*. I never doubted that this is a great book. It is theory, but it's also about creative teaching strategies for responding to children's different styles of learning. I was caught up with the reading, and it annoyed me to hear him repeat what I already knew. I could see that Nick was nervous, and, though it's my natural instinct to be supportive, and curious, I acted bored.

Mieke, taking over the lesson again, asked us to make two charts in order to see 12 though 25 and their squares as room numbers in two six-story buildings. Making trouble for her, I asked if I had to do my own: "I want to work with Alex on his chart." Mieke said okay, and I sat back and watched and didn't do any work. When I think about it now, my behavior was a far cry from what I expect from my third-grade students. It didn't dawn on me that, given how I was behaving, I could have been mistaken for Kenneth in Mrs. Smith's class the week before. Clearly, I wasn't catching on or interested.

It's not that my relationship with the other students in my group was usually unfriendly. I think we had all gotten to like each other, then and still, and we worked well together. During the lesson, Nakia was her usual studious self, following instructions, engrossed, and excited by the challenge. Dano, always very quiet because of his difficulty with English but always conscientious, when he wasn't answering a question from Mieke or Nick, had his pencil going the whole time. Alex and Pauli, who are both ready to follow any interesting tangent, paid attention when I didn't bother them. Later, Mieke said she was upset because some of us seemed bored, and I'm sure these same feelings contributed to Nick's nervousness. I feel badly now that my Superteacher self interfered with their teaching me. I guess because we had built up trust for each other, nobody complained about how I acted that day.

My difficulty isn't remembering what the teachers asked us to do. The problem is, because I had tuned out and wouldn't participate, I didn't learn many of the squares. Jerry has to fill in these details.)

Part 2. At this point, it might be helpful to create a mental structure that summarizes the whole task. What I recommend is to imagine two six-story buildings with one to three rooms on each floor. One building houses the "room" numbers to be squared, the teens on the first three floors and the twenties on the three above. The room numbers in the other building are the squares. Bold numbers, in both, indicate the squares that we've covered so far. This is building number one:

Floor		Rooms		
Sixth		25		
Fifth	23		24	
Fourth	20	21		22
Third		18	19	
Second	15	16	17	
First	12	13	14	

Identically shaped, though here the hundreds in the room numbers indicate the floors, is building number two:

```
                  6 - -
          5 - -            5 7 6
   4 - -           4 4 1            4 - -
          3 - -            3 - -
   2 - -           2 - -            2 - -
   1 4 4           1 6 9            1 9 6
```

What I picture are buildings that are essentially three rooms wide with balconies on each side of the two third-floor rooms and a sloping, peaked roof up from there. If a person can visualize these buildings, it is possible to readily know what hundred each square is—even if one doesn't know the exact answer.

This is how I have gone about learning these squares, and, of course, it isn't necessarily a useful method for everyone. If it doesn't seem useful, ignore my advice. Some students, children and adults, insist that they would rather stick with repetition because it is familiar. I say, go for it. My goal, as the teacher, is for students to learn in ways that are effective for them, and maybe these more creative approaches will crop up in the process. The task at hand is to learn five more squares by whatever method works best for a person. The numbers I suggest for part 2 are 15, 16, 17, 23, and 25. For me, they include all three rooms on the second floor, the one remaining room on the fifth, and the only one on the sixth.

We'll start with the two easy squares: $15 \times 15 = 225$ and $25 \times 25 = 625$. They are often already known by people, and, if not, they are usually not difficult to remember. Without an image of the buildings, one can relate the simple multiplication of $5 \times 5 = 25$ to the last two digits in these numbers, even though this isn't how the arithmetic actually works. Then, knowing that these squares are located on the second and sixth floors, it is possible to recognize them as the first of the 200s and the only 600. It's funny sometimes what contortions we'll go through to aid memory. In this case though, little help is probably needed to remember that the square of 15 is 225 and the square of 25 is 625.

In contrast, $16 \times 16 = 256$ and $17 \times 17 = 289$, the two squares of medium difficulty, do require some work. However, identifying two patterns makes it possible to know the answers readily without undue mental effort. The task is initially simplified if one knows that, of the squares of 15 through 17, 16 and 17 are the last of the 200s. Second, notice that the two pairs of numbers following the hundreds run in a broken sequence: 5 6 8 9. If the exact sequence isn't recalled, one can multiply 6×6 or 7×7 and see that the squares end in 6 and 9. Just knowing that there is a broken sequence involved, 56 89, either of these numbers, the 6 or the 9, is a good hint to nudge a sluggish memory into recalling that the square of 16 is 256 and the square of 17 is 289.

For the fifth and last square in part 2, I opt for tackling $23 \times 23 = 529$. This was a hard square for me to learn because I never came up with any surefire creative ideas for remembering it. When I say this, students are sometimes challenged to help me. My appearance as a student seems to bring out the aspiring teachers in them. The best image, so far, is 23 large hotel room keys with 529 embossed along the top. As a tease, the picture is supposed to remind me of all the hotel keys I've ever walked off with in my life and never returned. The square of 23 (keys) is 529 (on each).

It may not be necessary, but it is possible to conclude the second part of the lesson by visualizing these squares on an orange orange. Having two very different colored oranges in mind would contrast this set of five squares with the first one. Try it. Imagine, in place of "Sunkist" curving along the bottom, the square of 15 is 225, of 16 is 256, of 17 is 289. Above them, visualize the square of 25 is 625. Now, rotate the image in your mind and, on the blank back of the orange, squeeze in a picture of 23 keys for hotel room 529. Or put some image of your own on the back for the square of 23—maybe 20 keys on the orange and 3 falling off.

Take a break before going on to part 3.

(I talked with Greg, Benjamin, and Kenneth about the help I have been giving them. These kids are fascinated with me. The whole class itself seems to be taken with my presence. I wonder if it's because they all know my sons Colin, who is in fifth grade, and Trevor, who is in this class with them; or because I'm the only black man in school in the role of a teacher; or maybe a little bit of both.

I also talked with Mrs. Smith about Kenneth. She told me that he is new in school. He recently came from Kenya and has language problems—not the disadvantaged black kid I had assumed he was. She feels that he is shy, and she is worried because he is behind in reading, writing, and arithmetic. All three Rs!

My conversation with Mrs. Smith made more sense out of what I learned about Kenneth while talking with the boys. He is soft spoken but assured me that the multiplication chart helps him remember his tables. Moreover, he did not seem shy when I asked him some questions about the social studies assignment. He really warmed up to me. He had good answers, even though when I asked him to write them down, he only wrote incomplete sentences. The rest of the class does move at a rapid pace compared with him. Still, I think he is very bright.

Pondering these conversations, I was struck by similarities between Kenneth and me. I don't believe that our problems with multiplication are the same, yet I have to wonder whether, in common for us, something about these multiplication tables isn't meaningful. This is the crux of my disinterest. As an adult, I didn't see any point in memorizing the squares from 12 to 25. It didn't seem important to me, so I didn't take the assignment seriously—complicating matters further by rationalizing that it was the teachers' fault for not getting me involved in the lesson. I don't have any answers for Kenneth, but I do have more insight into thinking about what his difficulties might be.

My own discomfort was highest when Nick concluded the lesson with two questions. He wanted each of us to come up with some of our own creative ideas for teaching multiplication. Then, he asked the group how teaching strategies for the two-sided mind could be applied to other subjects. Nakia suggested the use of metaphors for remembering multiplication tables. I spent my energy arguing with her about how metaphors can't be applied to learning math. Alex pulled us away from the argument by mentioning that he especially liked visualizations. He thought they could be applied to teaching anything. Dano agreed with him because he knew for himself how much he depends on images when he is studying. Until class was over, I silently moped while the rest of the group discussed ideas that were interesting to me. It was dumb, but I told myself that I didn't care.)

Time to get back to work.

Part 3. Only four more squares to go. One of them is $20 \times 20 = 400$. It's the simplest of the fourteen squares, and hints for remembering it aren't needed. Therefore, there are only three to go: another easy one, the square of 22 (the remaining room on the fourth floor), and two hard ones, the squares of 18 and 19 (the only two rooms, with the balconies, on the third floor).

Before going on, I want to mention a problem connected with this lesson—and Bryant's struggles. Teaching is most effective when what students have to learn is meaningful to them. Yet it is not unusual to have to teach subjects for which there is no initial interest. Nor is it uncommon to encounter resistance. My strategy is to tap students' curiosity as a way of engaging them in a task that is meant to be more fun than practical. I bank on motivation that stems from wondering whether it is possible to truly learn this multiplication table quickly with little effort. If students feel that memorizing these squares is a game, they are likely to stick with it.

Beginning the windup, $22 \times 22 = 484$. Noting several characteristics makes this square easy to learn. It has symmetry, it can be viewed as a building with a high tower in the center, it contains only even numbers, multiplying 2×2 suggests the 4s on either side, the 8 in the middle is 2×4, and, besides, of all the squares, 22 can be multiplied by itself in the head most readily. It's not hard to see that $(2 \times 22 = 44) + (20 \times 22 = 440) = 484$. By the time one finishes contemplating these ideas, it may be self evident that the square of 22 is 484.

But the lesson isn't over, and there is still some difficult learning left. I haven't been able to find any patterns in the relationship between $18 \times 18 = 324$ and $19 \times 19 = 361$. Nor is there anything about these two squares that makes them intrinsically memorable. Like the other more difficult squares, my advice is to create striking mental images that tend not to be forgotten. For example, I visualize the square of 19 as an umbrella with a 6 for the handle, a 3 on the left of it, and a 1 on the right. In my mind, this is 361. It helps that I know that the square of 19 is on the third floor of the buildings I imagine. It also helps to know that 9×9 ends in 1. After constructing this image and losing it several times, it has finally stuck in my brain. The image of an umbrella now is associated with the square of 19: 361.

Last but certainly not least, my quest for an image that highlights the square of 18 continues. Knowing that it begins with 3 (from the floor number) and ends with 4 (by multiplying 8×8), I might add that my memory is only in second gear (suggesting a 2) for this pair. Putting the numbers together, I find that the square of 18 is 324. I want something more interesting though, something that stays in my mind more powerfully, something that is vivid and maybe funny too. Nothing comes to mind. This can be a challenge for my students this coming semester. I'll ask them to come up with an image that really works for me.

Finally, as a way of keeping the three parts of the lesson separate, I suggest imagining that the blue orange and the orange orange are in a small wooden crate. Look at the crate, in your mind, from the top—with both oranges in it— and then bring one of the sides into focus. On this side, visualize the square of 18 is 324. Rotate the box a quarter turn to see that the square of 19 is 361. Slowly, go two more quarter turns to see that 20 is 400 and that 22 is 484.

To review, "take" the oranges out of the crate and examine them. With the blue orange, look for *12 is 144, 21 is 441, 13 is 169, 14 is 196,* and *24 is 576.* On the front of the orange orange, find *15 is 225, 16 is 256, 17 is 289,* and *25 is 625.* On the back, *23 is 529.* Return the oranges to the crate and look on the sides for *18 is 324, 19 is 361, 20 is 400,* and *22 is 484.* Once all the squares are seen in the mind's eye, the last job is to fill all fourteen of them into the second of the two buildings on a piece of paper. If this lesson is reviewed twice a day for the next few days and then again, once a week later and once a month later, this multiplication table, like any other, will be remembered for life.

(At the beginning of the next class, Jerry gave a two-minute quiz on the squares. When the time was up, I had four answers out of fourteen. Four! Everyone in class knows I'm a math major. At that moment, I felt shame, humility, failure, and God knows what else. I said to myself, "You pompous ass."

I came into the first class, all ego, totally sure of myself, convinced that the "Art and Science of Teaching" would be a breeze, with a Superteacher image. I've always been a leader. I never want to follow, and I'm never afraid to step up and grab a bull by the horns. And it's important to me how I am thought of by others. For once, what is usually too much time driving alone in my truck to and from the city, between school, work, and the Air Force Reserves, turned out to be a good thing. The rest of the day and through some of the night, I stewed and thought about what had happened.

I retreated into my journal, assigned to keep a record of each time we meet, and replayed the past weeks in my mind—starting from week one. I found out how much I had learned from my classmates. My mood on the day that Mieke and Nick were teaching didn't jive with what I had written in my journal on better days, and I recognized how I was learning as much from other students as I was from Jerry and the books. One time, I was "lecturing" Willie, a classmate in one of the other groups, a black woman whose name went with her common sense, on how the brothers have to get their acts together. Sure of my eloquence, I finally took a breath. She said, "Watch out for leading so far ahead; when you turn around, there's no one there."

Surprisingly, adjusting my attitude wasn't that difficult. It was made easier by the fact that everyone around me, including my own kids, was ready. In the weeks that followed, I was a willing student for the teachers who were responsible for the second theme, the emotional side of learning, and I was an appreciated teacher when it was my turn to guide the third theme, freedom in the classroom. I haven't lost my familiar self-confidence, but, certainly, my need for perfection, from myself and others, has been toned down. I can't say who else noticed, but my kids did. Out of Colin's mouth comes, "More human." "More understanding and listens to me better," says Trevor. There aren't more critical reviewers, so it must be true. By the end of the semester, I had a new image. . . .

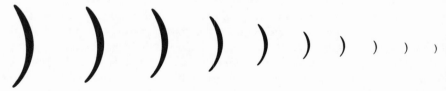

Look! Up in the air! It's a bird? It's a plane? No! It's Superteacher! Actually, it's still me, Bryant. I busted out of the parenthesis. I'm back to Superteacher— with my new image. Jerry and I agreed that it's up to me to tell you the rest.

First, a commercial. Be sure to do your homework before going on. Take it from me. You will be much more satisfied, happier, I would say, if you know all fourteen squares by the end of the story. And now, we return to the last exciting class. Actually, there are two of them.

I thought the last class at the Media School was the day we finished up my solo lesson. Unassisted by Mrs. Smith, I had taught the class how to make pyramids. The students learned how to use metric measures, historical facts about pyramids, and how to build them out of construction paper. To my surprise, Mrs. Smith called me at home later in the week and asked if I could come one more day so that the kids could say good-bye. We would have cookies and juice.

When I arrived, she sat me in the front of the room and gathered all of the children around me. Each one had written me a letter of appreciation for the time I had spent there. The children had made folders and had put the letters in along with drawings—mostly of pyramids. Mrs. Smith asked me to read them aloud, and I felt very special.

The children commented on what they had learned about pyramids. They also told me that I would be a great teacher. Their words felt sincere, and Kenneth touched me the most. He wrote a wonderful letter:

> *Dear Mr. Chavous,*
>
> *Good luck you are a great teacher you*
> *helped Me when I couldn't know*
> *what to do like how to Make pyramids. I will*
> *Miss you, Mr. Chavous.*
> > *Sincerely,*
> > *Kenneth*

Best of all, as if he knew about Superteacher's struggles, the folder, with a border on the cover of little books and glasses all the way around, had a title in the middle with big bold letters:

T h E   S K y's   T h E   L i m i t

My grandmother would say, "I got happy," which is the way Baptists describe someone experiencing a religious feeling overtaking the conscious self. I almost burst out in tears, and I'm not sure I did the right thing by holding back. The feeling of that day will stay with me the rest of my life. Any doubts I had about becoming a teacher are gone.

One last message from Superteacher. Don't forget, the secret password is . . . blue orange.

~

Take out a piece paper. In two minutes, write down as many squares from 12 to 25 as you can remember. Check your answers from the book. The highest score is fourteen.

9

Three Voices

JERRY'S STORY

I was annoyed with Dorian, Alexandria, and Khayyam for not taking this week's assignment seriously. Frankly, I felt they were blowing it off. To make matters worse, I was annoyed with myself. I hadn't done the assignment either. As part of feeling guilty, I was unwilling to imagine that our resistance was essentially the same.

It's a pet peeve of mine that teachers ask students to do work they have never done themselves. Not every semester, but certainly a teacher should have done the assignment at some point in time. I rationalized that writing stories for this book counted for my version of the assignment. But I knew better. I was asking the students to enter into and represent the voices of their elementary school students. So far, I'd only woven students' writing with my own. I had not taken on the challenge of actually writing a student's voice, from inside me, as the assignment required.

These students made up a subteam responsible for teaching their small group a lesson that incorporated this writing assignment, and I saw that they weren't doing an adequate job of preparing. Meanwhile, my guilt hounded me. One morning, after a fitful night, what I was to do was obvious. My assignment was to write their story in the way I was asking my students to write about their students.

In preparation, I reviewed their experience experiments, journals, and papers and chose Dorian to be the narrator. When I finished writing, I asked the three of them to read the story, and they told me that it conveyed the spirit and feelings of what really happened. With their permission, I shared the story the following semester with a new class of students. They said it helped them do the assignment. Best of all, Dorian, Alexandria, Khayyam, and I were left respecting each other.

DORIAN'S STORY

Finally. After two years of humdrum undergraduate college classes, except for math, Dorian was in her first education course. She loved math. Her feelings about teaching were not so clear, but by becoming a math teacher, she knew she could do what she loved. It was working out, too, that this first education course, now halfway through the semester, was intriguing. If only there weren't such annoying times.

One of the memorable ones took place early on. In the third week of class, Dorian and Professor Allender had a heated discussion. After a short lecture and several students talking about their tutoring in nearby schools, he asked for comments, his words mind you, "either positive or negative," about what the class had learned from applying concepts from the readings to the practical problems faced while teaching the children they were assigned. Dorian had been reading *Growing Minds* by Herbert Kohl, and she told Allender frankly that the book hadn't been helpful at all. He didn't seem too upset by this honest reaction, but he insisted that she discuss, in detail, their different understanding of Kohl's ideas. At the time, she hadn't finished reading the book, and several students who also got into the discussion assured her that she would change her mind by the end. Well, she didn't.

It was a week later when she finished Kohl in the wee hours of the morning. With too little sleep, she came to class in a bad mood. Then, Alexandria, Khayyam, and she were assigned to teach, for the week after next, a lesson on story writing to their small group. She hated writing. Last week's team had been assigned an intriguing math lesson, and now this!

"I'm so annoyed. Professor Allender tells us not to worry. He says, 'It's more challenging to teach a subject you don't know.' I really wanted to teach a math lesson. It is so unfair."

Dorian didn't get any disagreement from Alexandria: "A writing lesson, yuck! We both like math, and we're not given any choice."

Quietly, Khayyam offered his opinion, "Actually, I like this assignment. It's better than math for me."

Professor Allender took them and the other subteams aside to explain what they had to do to cover the emotional side of learning, the new theme.

"At the end of this week, collect the papers I assigned on writing a short story about a tutoring experience using a student's voice. With these in hand, plan a discussion that relates the papers and the readings to the questions listed in the syllabus and any of your own. Remember, though, it's particularly important for you to first write the paper yourselves. It's a pet peeve of mine that teachers ask students to do work they have never done themselves.

"Plan for an hour. Start with a *short* lecture about how the two books, *The Education of Little Tree* by Forrest Carter and *Spinning Inward* by Maureen Murdock, help us to understand the emotional side of learning, and end the lesson with a discussion of how these ideas can be applied in the schools where you are now tutoring. In the middle, for most of the time, plan two or three activities, using ideas from the books and the papers you've collected. Get your students actively interested and involved."

Dorian's hand snapped up: "Professor Allender, do we get class time for planning too?" She pointed out that the teams who had taught the math lesson had gotten time at the end of class for the whole week before they had to teach.

"Sure," he said, "twenty to thirty minutes before the end of class next week. I'll assist each team in turn. And I hope you will set up at least one meeting outside of class."

During the following week, they had three planning meetings—except Alexandria missed the first one and Khayyam missed the third. Dorian and Khayyam alone didn't get much done. They mostly chatted while hoping Alexandria would show up late as she had done on several occasions, and then, finally, there was only time to clarify the assignment for themselves.

At the beginning of the second meeting, Dorian couldn't help herself from taking over. She jumped in before anyone said a word. "We need to divide up the work so that each of us knows what to do. Khayyam, you are the only one of us who picked *The Education of Little Tree* to read. You'll have to do something that relates that book to the lesson. I found a number of interesting imagery activities in *Spinning Inward*. Alexandria and I can choose ones that we like from them. What we need now is an overall plan. We have to fit all of the pieces together."

Alexandria, who was a returning older student with two children and an elderly mother living with her, started by apologizing for missing the first meeting: "I'm really sorry. Everything was falling apart at home. The kids were both sick, my mother needed medicine from the drugstore, and I don't want to tell you the rest. I'm lucky to be here today."

Dorian pushed ahead, "I hope your life eases up at home, but we better get going. Khayyam, have you thought about how *Little Tree* could fit in? What's it about?"

"It's a story of an orphan, a young boy named Little Tree, who lives with his Cherokee grandparents in a mountain cabin. They have to teach him because there isn't any school. I like the book."

"Is it true?" Alexandria asked.

"Professor Allender," Khayyam answered, "says some people think it is and some not. Either way, it shows you how Little Tree learned to read, and write, and do arithmetic, and lots of other things, without going to school. It sounds like a nice way to grow up."

Dorian asked, "Could you tell the story and lead a discussion about the book?"

"I don't know. The students who already read it might not want to hear it again."

"I guess that's a problem."

Alexandria suggested, "Why don't you pick out just a couple interesting parts to retell and lead a discussion about them?"

"That's a great idea," said Dorian.

They agreed that this is what should be done. For their next meeting, Dorian and Alexandria promised to pick out one or two imagery activities from *Spinning Inward* that could be applied to the lesson. Then they went on to look at the papers they had collected.

From their five students, they had gotten only three papers—the others weren't finished yet—and only two of their own—because Khayyam hadn't done his either. The one from Stacie revealed how excited her kindergarten children were about preparing for Halloween. Abby told a funny story about two first-grade kids who were misbehaving and what they were feeling and thinking. They glanced at the other papers but ran out of time and decided to leave the rest for their last meeting.

They were to get together the next afternoon in the student lounge. Khayyam called Dorian at home that morning to say that his football coach had called an early practice and he wouldn't be able to make the meeting.

"Don't worry," he told her, "I'll have my part ready, and it will be easy to work it in."

Dorian groaned inwardly, "I don't believe this is happening!" With effort, she thanked Khayyam for calling.

Later, that afternoon, she felt better while meeting with Alexandria. The two of them decided exactly how the lesson would go from beginning to end, and it wasn't that difficult to fit Khayyam's piece into the plan. In fact, it felt easier planning without him there.

They decided on two questions about the stories that the students had written: How did the teacher-student relationship help learning? And did it hinder in any way? Dorian would introduce the lesson and then lead a guided fantasy about their teaching experiences. Alexandria's job was to ask the students to answer the two questions. They agreed that Khayyam would end the lesson with a discussion comparing Little Tree's experiences with those of their students.

The day to teach arrived. Soon after getting to class, however, Dorian had a distinct feeling that this was going to be another particularly bad day.

Professor Allender had already taken care of the administrative details, and the schedule was on the blackboard. There was going to be a short discussion about problems they faced while tutoring in the schools. At the same time, though, those who were scheduled to teach their small groups this period were being excused to set up mini classrooms in the hall and do last-minute preparation. Dorian was very distressed. The extra time was appreciated by all the teachers—except Alexandria and Khayyam, who hadn't appeared yet.

"What good is the time if they're not here?" she practically screamed out loud. More than this, only two other members of her group, those who would be her students, had shown up so far. In a class full of friendly people, she was alone.

Before Professor Allender began the discussion, he walked over to Dorian. Maybe, she fantasized, he was going to tell her that she wouldn't have to teach today. He didn't. Instead, "I've got bad news for you. Just before class began, Khayyam's roommate came to tell me that he is sick and won't be in class. The good news is that he brought the notes that Khayyam wrote on the *Education of Little Tree* for you and Alexandria to use for his part of the lesson."

Though Dorian only stamped her foot in her mind, she didn't hide her frustration: "I don't believe this is happening to me!"

Professor Allender consoled her, "You've got Khayyam's notes. They might be useful. Think of this as the same as any day when a teacher you are working with is absent. It will be practice for a realistic situation."

Dorian was near to tears: "You don't understand. Alexandria isn't here either, nor are Sherry and both Stacey's. That leaves me with no teachers to teach with and only two students."

Professor Allender paused for a long minute. "Maybe they'll come late. I understand this is difficult for you, but I still want you to do the best you can under the circumstances." He left her to talk with another student.

At best, Dorian was mixed up. She was angry, anxious, resigned, determined, and most of all frustrated. She slowly walked to the area in the hall assigned to her group. Of all of the areas, it was the best space. Although it was close to the elevators, there were two couches in an alcove, in the shape of an L, and extra chairs that could be used to close in the other two sides to form a small circle. After staring at the elevator doors for a while, she let herself be comforted by the pleasant makeshift classroom and began to read Khayyam's notes.

They were difficult to understand, hard to read, and confusing. Dorian couldn't figure out how he had intended to use them. Hopeless, her mind turned to other worries.

"And if Alexandria doesn't come, how am I going to teach by myself? How can there be a discussion with only two students? I know what'll happen if I get nervous. My mind will go blank. I won't remember what I was trying to say. This is the reason I decided to become a math teacher. In math, it's clear what has to be taught, and one doesn't have to depend on students' opinions. Is Alexandria even going to show up?"

She saw Professor Allender coming down the hall with Abby and Angie, her two students, trailing behind. She felt as if she were waking up to a bad day all over again. He announced, "It's time to start your class." As Abby and Angie were sitting down, he took Dorian aside: "This is a difficult situation, but there are a couple of things I want to tell you. First, your lesson isn't graded on how successful it is. The requirement is only to teach a lesson, whatever the result, and learn from the experience. Second, however long the lesson lasts will be good enough. If you run out of what to do, find me, and I'll help you wind up the discussion. Can you manage?"

Dorian murmured, "Sure," and Allender went off to get the other groups started.

As she was turning back to her students, the elevator doors facing the alcove opened as if they were a dramatic scene in a movie. Swoosh. Alexandria stepped into the hall, directly across, looking sheepish. Seeing her, after a sigh, Dorian smiled with relief—which was immediately followed by a smile on Alexandria's face. To the students, Dorian said with authority, "Find something to keep yourselves busy; class won't begin for another five minutes."

The two teachers hurriedly conferenced. Alexandria learned of Khayyam's absence and looked over his notes. "I don't think I'll have any problem leading his part of the discussion. I'm ready to begin any time you are."

Dorian's mood was mostly up from there. Abby and Angie were delighted with imagining they were pilots of a spaceship traveling to Earth. Abby, tickled with the fantasy, played with levers, knobs, and gizmos to control her spaceship on its way. They visited the classrooms where their stories took place and looked back on their tutoring experiences as would someone from another planet. Sharing their memories, the students together with Alexandria and Dorian had a fun, actually sometimes funny, discussion.

Alexandria asked the students to read the stories they had written out loud. There were lots of excited suggestions for how the stories might be rewritten to better understand the motivation, interest, and involvement of their students. They wondered about understanding students' feelings. Alexandria raised a tough question: "Can a person learn to have empathy?"

Alexandria plowed right on into a discussion of Little Tree. It didn't take long before she confirmed Dorian's suspicion that Khayyam's notes were a total mess. What Alexandria was saying hardly made sense. Dorian was getting frustrated again, so she didn't hesitate to interrupt. As Dorian explained later, "I decided to make life easier for the both of us. That's why I asked Abby and Angie if they had read the book."

Angie had, and Abby was up to the last chapter. Dorian paused and said, "You tell us how the book is related to our lesson." They were delighted to talk about Little Tree and his grandparents. The stories they told made them all laugh and once almost cry. What touched them was how Little Tree managed to survive the brutal boarding school he was forced to attend when he was taken from his grandparents. Just before the time ran out, Dorian asked, "How do Little Tree's experiences compare with our students?" They agreed that it was hard to compare, but they did realize that a teacher can unwittingly cause a student to suffer.

When class was over, Dorian and Alexandria stayed behind to talk.

"You don't need to tell me why you were late. I am glad you got here."

Alexandria blushed, "Me too."

They laughed about how plans never go the way you plan. Dorian admitted that a teacher has to learn how to improvise, even though the idea made her nervous. "You know," she said as they were leaving, "talking about stories from a student's point of view actually improves my mood."

Alexandria nodded, "Me too. It makes me think about Khayyam. It has to be tough to be a football player and a college student at the same time. I hope he makes out all right."

HOLLIE'S STORY (written the following semester by Hollie Gilchrist)

Dorian and I are similar. We both found a way to be comfortable in class. The big difference was our struggle. At this point in the semester, her frustration came from the classmates who disappointed her. I became aware that I was disappointed with myself.

As far I was concerned, this was a killer course. You really had to think to get through it, not only about the materials but also about yourself, and until we began studying about the emotional side of learning, I wasn't ready to think about myself.

This was not what I expected when I enrolled. Dorian was certainly annoyed at times, but it was the very first moment I walked into class and saw a circle of chairs that my heart sank. All I could think was, "Oh no, a discussion class!" The first few weeks confirmed how horrible the course was. To begin, the teacher walked in, sat down, and wanted us to know everyone's name. We had to choose a book from a list of seven, go to a school and tutor, do an experience experiment, and write a paper—for the second week! The third week we had to *draw* the experience experiment. As I saw it, for me, too shy for my own good, pressed with work from all of my classes, and without artistic talent, this was a nightmare, and I was going to fail.

I adjusted. When we were meeting as a large group and Jerry was lecturing, asking questions, or leading a discussion, it was possible to hide in the crowd. As the unexpected became expected, weird activities like holding hands and passing a squeeze around a circle to help us learn each others' names felt less weird. The assignments, my classmates, and the professor, who initially felt too far out, all eventually began to feel, not great, but okay.

Wouldn't you know it, though, after a while I started getting uncomfortable again. But this time it came from something bothering me inside. I was no longer content to sit quietly. I didn't talk, and at the same time I wanted to. Ever since grade school, where my teachers used me as an example of the smart girl in class, I have felt self-conscious about speaking up. I was always afraid that the other kids would tease me and call me names. The fear grew. I went through all of high school without ever volunteering an answer in class, and I wasn't any different my first year in college.

Becoming a sophomore didn't make me think I would change. Yet the atmosphere of this class pushed me to open up. I have to believe that it had to do with how Jerry taught the class. It's funny, though, that's not what I recall. It's the people in my group that stand out in my mind. They were the ones who encouraged me to talk.

My secret hero was Vince. From the beginning of the semester, the strangest things came out of his mouth. The first time was when Jerry asked us to give six students feedback. They had come up to the blackboard to explain the visual aids we had drawn in our small groups. In the discussion, there were compliments and constructive criticisms. Then everyone was quiet. Jerry called on the people who hadn't spoken and asked them individually if they wanted to say anything. After a few additional opinions, and a few of us who said no, Jerry says, "Vince?" And Vince says, after hesitating a moment, "I think they were boring!" There was a loud silence in class.

Jerry handled it all right. He pushed on him to be specific, and Vince wasn't totally negative. In fact, though it seemed that most students were disagreeing, much of what he said made sense to me. After that, we could always count on Vince to say something shocking.

Including Vince, there were seven of us, and Heather, Lavell, and I were the first to plan a lesson for the group. We had to teach the others the squares of 12 to 25. We were confused when the task was first explained, but after a week and a half of planning, the lesson went well. We used creative teaching techniques; the students thought they were fun, and so did we. Although I'm not certain, it was probably when the three of us were planning together that I got this bug to talk in class. Because we were only three, while we were planning together, I had to participate. With no place to hide, staying quiet was too awkward.

Heather, full of excitement and energy, was talkative and never at a loss for words. Luckily, after telling us what she thought, she was also willing to hear our opinions. Lavell was soft-spoken, serious, and concerned about inner-city schools. Though typically quiet, because he more often than not disagreed with her, he too always had something to say. After him, it was natural for me to speak. I was never without thoughts, so I said what was on my mind. Even when we misunderstood each other, it was especially nice that we were all willing to listen. The listening part was familiar and enjoyable to me, and talking didn't feel as bad as I feared. I guess once I got started, I didn't want to stop.

The time came for Vince and his partner, Kecia, to teach the group about the emotional side of learning. We gathered in our alcove. It sure wasn't as nice as Dorian's: the middle and the rear ceiling lights were burned out, and the further back you were, the dingier it got. There were abandoned file cabinets and two broken chairs sitting askew along the rear wall. All that was missing were cobwebs to complete the image. We had a big rectangular table, though, where we could all sit together.

The group sat around three sides, and across from us, a couple of feet away, Kecia and Vince leaned on an old desk. It was pushed up against the wall, and they were looking at their notes and talking too quietly for us to hear. While waiting for them, we were talking too—except I was mostly thinking. I was busy shaking my head wondering about Vince's craziness. Kecia was an interesting, practical person and sane. It was easy to imagine her as a teacher, but Vince?

I also thought, This could be a blast. Two weeks before, Kecia told me that she was not looking forward to planning with Vince. "Why me?" she asked. She was worried about the plans for their teaching because he didn't seem to agree with anyone. A week later, she felt better. She said Jerry had given them some good ideas. After that, she didn't say anything about the lesson; she just smiled. I think Vince had gotten to her. Kecia stood and tapped a pencil on the table to get our attention.

"Listen up. We're going to get started. Vince and I brought sunglasses for everyone to wear. We couldn't afford regular ones, so we bought kiddy glasses at a toy store." As she is handing them out, she tells us, "Put them on. They'll help you with the visualization activity we're going to do."

Sitting there in the hall with the glasses on, I felt like an idiot. Two students from another class walked by and stared at us. It was embarrassing. I wished Kecia and Vince hadn't been so cooperative as students when Lavell, Heather, and I were teaching. Then I wouldn't have had to do the same for them.

What happened surprised me. The beginning of the lesson wasn't a whole lot different than what happened in Dorian's story. We didn't go on a spaceship, but we did visualize—with help from Kecia and our magic glasses—our teaching experiences. This brought up the first problem. I was the only one who did the third experience experiment right. Fred hadn't gotten it done at all. The others hadn't followed the assignment. They found it too difficult to write a story about how their students felt, so they turned in regular reports.

Our second problem was talking. Not too much, but too little. Vince was leading the discussion, and it was tough. Normally, we were a very talkative group, but without Heather, who was absent, and with Kecia and Vince doing the teaching, we discovered that the other five of us were the quiet ones. It just never had been noticeable before because the three of them were always ready to fill in the silences. Vince was not happy, and you could see him plotting.

"Hollie," he says to me—and then there is his usual hesitation before he opens his mouth again—"you wrote a story about your students. Tell the group what happened like you were one of the kids." Funny, a month ago I would have died. At that moment, I was eager and ready.

I took a deep breath and out came, "Okay . . . the teacher is Miss Gilchrist. My name is Judy, and I'm the narrator.

"Kevin, Mallory, Andrew, and I were kind of nervous about volunteering for the extra writing assignment, but we liked when Miss Gilchrist helped us with our lessons. Besides, we were going to get extra credit.

"Miss Gilchrist told us that we were going to go on an imaginary adventure, and she gave us three choices: 'Friendship on a Deserted Island,' 'Time Travel,' or 'An Undersea Journey.' Mallory and I wanted to do the friendship one. Kevin and Andrew wanted to go under the sea. We talked about it, and Mallory and I convinced them that the deserted island would be more fun. We told them we could make up strange kinds of animals and have an erupting volcano—like the one we learned about in our science class. When the boys heard the words *erupting volcano*, they were sold.

"At first, I thought that Miss Gilchrist was really weird. She asked us to close our eyes and pay attention to our breathing. We were not supposed to think about anything else. It made me even more nervous to think about somebody looking at me and making fun of me while my eyes were closed. She said it was okay just to stare at the wall. We giggled."

Judy kept right on talking. She told how Miss Gilchrist asked them, while paying attention to their breathing, to let out bad feelings and worries each time they exhaled, to then imagine being on a deserted island with a best friend, and afterward to describe their islands. She described an island with pools of water and lots of seashells, her best friend Brittany, how funny she was, how they made necklaces out of the seashells, and how that was the best part. She went on about their writing assignment—to describe the flowers, the trees, the animals, and the foods they encountered, with attention to colors, sounds, smells, and tastes. Judy didn't leave out how Miss Gilchrist said something about textures and that she didn't know what that meant.

I didn't quit talking until my group heard about Mallory's island with talking animals and an orange and purple sky; the boys' islands full of alligators, monkeys, and erupting volcanoes; and how BORING! the girls thought the boys' islands were. The story ended with Judy thinking that this was the best story she had ever written. She hoped it would be published—which meant it would be sent to the principal as an example of good work from her class.

When I finally took my second breath, everyone laughed. Vince smiled and said my story was pretty good too, but he wasn't going to send it to the principal. The group laughed a second time. When Vince tried to get the discussion going, though, it was still tough. Breaking the silence after a long pause, somebody said something that struck a nerve. Although I don't remember who it was or what it was, it was like a flood had just broken a barrier inside of me, and the words kept coming, and I wasn't worrying over what anyone thought about how much I talked. I realized that I had many things to say about my experiences all through school. I went right on talking. The best part was that everyone was listening to me, and I knew they wouldn't criticize. For the first time since grade school, I was comfortable enough with myself and the people around me to let loose and speak my mind. I felt great!

~

Two weeks later, the turn to teach fell on Janelle and another Heather in our group. The assignment this time was to lead a panel discussion in front of the whole class. They were the moderators, and the others of us in the group were the panel. I felt sorry because they were even shyer than I was. I didn't believe they could do it. As it turned out, I didn't need to feel sorry. Though they had hardly participated in Vince and Kecia's lesson, they clearly had learned some lessons of their own.

They led a great panel discussion. To lead it off, they both spoke personally. Janelle explained how her Caribbean accent made her self-conscious. She hadn't been in the United States very long, and she was generally shy in the first place.

Heather, to my surprise, told us how she too had become afraid in grade school of answering questions, even though she knew the answers, because she didn't want to be labeled a brain or a nerd. She was exactly like me! After their introduction, everyone in our group wanted to talk, and the two of them could hardly keep the rest of the class, which was the audience, from chiming in out of turn.

10

The Structure of Freedom in the Classroom

Coming up are four thirty-minute panel discussions addressing the theme "Freedom in the Classroom." Though my past experience with student-led panel discussions has been good enough, often exciting and entertaining, I am not fully satisfied with the level of learning that occurs. The problems chosen for discussion are usually highly controversial and unlikely to uncover even the beginnings of practical solutions. They lead to impassioned arguments in which voices are raised and listening is low. Students are not empowered to face the more common problems, plentiful enough, that confront a teacher everyday. I want more understanding.

So, this week my biggest concern is with the quality of listening. An important part is, of course, hearing the words that are spoken. However, the other part of paying attention to someone's ideas and concerns is responding in a way that makes the person feel heard. It is difficult enough for a teacher to insist that children be quiet when it is someone's turn to talk. It is still more difficult to lead a discussion in a way that keeps the attention on the student who spoke, recognizing that the turn is not over until he or she feels understood. A teacher should not want to discourage open discussion; still, gentle guidance is needed for this kind of listening.

I hope that modifying the structure of the panels will better achieve my goals. During the last two weeks, the students learned this structure and practiced it as well. The presentation leaders had to decide who would be the moderator and side persons. They had to make sure that the rest of the students in their group were knowledgeable about the book they had chosen to read and about questions they might have to answer. They also had to figure out how they would invite the audience, the other students in the class, to participate.

To help them prepare, I handed out a questionnaire entitled "Panel Notes." Their answers would give the moderators a range of material about which to ask questions—questions the panel members have already had a chance to think about. The "Panel Notes" are meant to insure that the moderators and panel members show themselves in a good light. I want each person on the panel to feel like an expert so that the questions and answers will lead to a lively and interactive class discussion. I am hoping that the discussion will clarify connections among the readings, tutoring experiences, and their personal reflections.

After nearly a whole semester of lectures and group activities, questions and discussions, and challenging tutoring experiences in local schools, I thought that these panels were an easy way to review and explore the work that we have done so far. Yet it was a difficult assignment. The resistance began the day I met with the leaders of the four panels. It helped a little that a few of them had already filled out the "Panel Notes," but there was a general sense that leading a panel, or even being on a panel, was foreign territory.

I handed them a three-page lesson plan, a page of specifics on what a discussion of freedom in the classroom might look like, and a page of ideas on how to prepare their groups for being on a panel. I also gave them a completed version of the "Panel Notes," including a favorite story from one of the books, a biggest concern that I have right now about being a good teacher, and two questions that I was prepared to answer.

There wasn't time to read the handouts carefully at this meeting, and my explanations and our discussion seemed to both mollify and exacerbate their confusion. I assured everyone that the assignment would be clearer by the time we met again at the end of the next class, and I pointed out that there was a week and a half before the panels were scheduled to begin. My teacherly delusion was that they would be enthusiastic because it seemed to be such a wonderful opportunity. That idea I had to give up, but they seemed motivated at least not to look foolish. It was good enough for the moment.

In general, the panel discussions are difficult for me too. It is more than ever the time in the course when students should be encouraged to do what they want to do, and yet I have such clear images of how the theme should be discussed and, of greater importance to me, what it means to listen carefully to each other. I have worked at influencing the panel leaders while they were planning. They paid heed to the extent that what I had to say made the task more comfortable. Mainly though, they kept to their own track, choosing the important questions and the style that would be best for leading a panel. Because I am concerned about freedom in my own classroom, I was willing to back off. I also know that once the panels begin, I will not allow myself to voice opinions except when I am called on as a member of the audience—and even then not too often. To achieve what I want, I have to be quiet. The challenge is to create the structure and trust the process.

FIRST PANEL

Moderator: Chari
Side Person and Wrap-Up: Josh
Panel Members: Jill, Jamie M., Lori M., and Roxanne

Between Chari and Josh, their choosing who would be the moderator wasn't difficult. Chari had been very talkative all semester long. It was a good thing, and it was a problem. Whenever I asked for questions or comments, I could count on Chari. For sure, her hand, waving, would go up, and usually she just started in. In all fairness, I intentionally encouraged students to speak freely without raising their hands, and besides, what she had to say was interesting and thought provoking. On the other hand, her uninhibited responses, echoed by her friend in another group, seemed to inhibit others from speaking, particularly students who were generally quiet. But she was a natural for the moderator job.

Josh, however, was a character—by reputation and by his own unabashed description. One day, for example, he was wearing a long key chain attached to his pants. The end with the keys fell down the back of his chair. As he struggled to free the key chain and himself from the chair, he stood, and the hold between them became fast. So he and the chair scraped across the floor.

Later, in his journal, Josh wrote about the incident, "I like the structure of this class. It goes quickly for me, and it is interesting. But I intentionally disrupt the class when it gets boring. I can't help it. It's part of my personality to be the center of attention, and this is why I think I'll make a good teacher." And this is probably why Josh, as the side person, became the more figural leader of the panel.

Chari organized the "Panel Notes." She was attracted to the most prevalent concerns: student teachers worrying about connecting with their students' interests, developing sensitivity to children's needs, assuring comprehension of the content, having control without losing patience, and having fun and being assertive at the same time. She was sure that questions about such concerns would apply to everyone. If there were awkward silences, Chari knew too that she could offer her own opinions. With these, she was always ready.

It wasn't so easy for Josh. He worried. For him, the assignment dealt with the aspect of teaching that he feared the most—being the authority. Never in his life was he the authority—not at home, not at school, and not in any of the jobs that he had held. He told me about his fears, and I attempted to minimize them by suggesting that in small ways everyone has experienced exercising some authority. "What about your expertise as a class clown?" I asked. He laughed. I added, "Because you are the wrap-up person and only a backup for the moderator, at least you have the less difficult leadership role. It's a way to ease yourself in."

On the scheduled Monday, each of the panelists sat in a chair along the front blackboard. The students on the other panels sat across from them in a semicircle along the back and side walls. Chari and Josh sat next to each other in chairs that were on an angle out from the blackboard, permitting them to easily face both the panelists and the audience.

As they waited for the class to get settled, Chari was confident and Josh was nervous. They had asked me if they could go first. Josh wanted to get it over

with, and that was fine with Chari. She began by welcoming the class and introducing each member of the panel. Her first question, as she had planned, addressed concerns about being a good teacher. There was a long pause, but it
wasn't too long before Roxanne braved an answer. And then, with short silences
in between, the others answered too.

It didn't surprise me that Chari was in charge and Josh didn't say much. When
Chari asked about reactions to the readings, though, there was a change. Josh
seemed to light up. While in front of the class for these few minutes listening to
the conversation, he had become comfortable enough to try out being in charge.
When Jamie raised her hand, he called on her before Chari got a word in.

Though Jamie had read *Freedom to Learn* by Carl Rogers and Jerome Freiberg
in preparation for the panel discussion, she wanted to comment on *Totto-chan*.
"This wasn't the book I chose, but I've heard a lot about it in class discussions.
From what I gather, freedom to learn in the primary grades worked well. But this
was a special kind of school in Japan with only ten or so kids in each class. In
America, we have twenty-five to thirty-five children in our classes to keep under
control. I fear children walking out of class anytime they want—to go to the
bathroom, to get a drink, to visit other teachers or other kids. I feel this is a
waste of the students' and the teacher's precious time."

Josh was his goofy self. He made a funny face at Jamie and said, "You didn't
read the book?!" He looked at the panel, paused, raised his voice slightly, and
out came, "What do *you* think of her opinion?"

Jill dove in. "I agree with Jamie. Every child needs some type of freedom, but
too much can be hazardous. I believe that children should be allotted a certain
amount of time everyday or one day out of the week to explore and have some
freedom. The other time in the classroom should be structured. Without structure, things have a tendency to get out of hand."

Kevin, who was in the audience, waved at Josh, and he was called on next.

"Freedom in the classroom is beneficial for keeping students interested. Most
classes are way too boring. Freedom adds spice to the class and gives it some
flavor."

Josh was about to call on the next person, but Chari interrupted, "Before we
get a big discussion going, I think we have to hear from all of the panel members
first."

Now that Josh was started, there was no stopping him. He picked right up on
Chari's suggestion. "Lori and Roxanne, what are your opinions?"

The two of them tended to be quiet, but Lori was ready to answer. "To tell
you the truth, I don't have an opinion. In fact, I'm having so much trouble with
the little first-grade boy I'm tutoring, I'm beginning to dread going to my school
every week. I go there, and I come home with a headache, and I'm really tired
of coming home with a headache. He can hardly write, and it seems like he isn't
getting any better. I find it a waste of my time to try helping him. I don't know
if freedom or structure would help. He has so many problems at home."

Josh and Chari both looked at Roxanne. She spoke softly, "I don't know either. In the first few weeks of this course, I have to admit I was really uncomfortable with the style of this class. I was used to assigned seats, strict due dates, lectures, and tests. I even thought of it as an 'easy course.' But as time went on, I discovered that though there were no strict rules, I still had to think. I appreciate that Jerry is willing to share his power, but I don't know yet how I'm going to do that."

After this, it wasn't difficult to keep the discussion going. Other ideas came up around the question of freedom or structure which actually prevented Chari from using all of the questions she had prepared. She happily commented, though, on most everyone else's questions and opinions, and Josh was content to call on whomever was ready with something to say. When there was a silence, he said something funny or made a goofy face.

In his final paper, Josh wrote, "Leading the panel was good practice for when I become a teacher with a classroom of my own. I learned that getting students' respect is as important as giving them the respect they deserve. With this in mind, I shouldn't have trouble being an authority figure in my classroom."

SECOND PANEL

Moderator: Erika
Side Person and Wrap-Up: Janice
Panel Members: Kenyatta M. and Candice

Erika was another class character. She wasn't overly talkative, but when she wanted to be, she was bold, almost fearless, and seemed to be willing to say anything on her mind. Early on in the semester, I felt uncomfortably confronted by her several times when she complained or disagreed with me—and sometimes she even seemed to be poking at me indirectly when challenging others. My tendency is to simplify these kinds of conflicts by finding common ground between myself and the student or by helping students to find such connections between each other. After a couple of tries, I realized this approach wasn't working, and I knew I would have to be more creative.

My immediate option was to listen more carefully. When Erika spoke, I was especially attentive and willing to spend a greater amount of time focusing on what she was saying and how others were responding. My attempts appeared successful, and for sure, I was happier with the flow of the discussions for everyone involved.

A riskier option was to ask Erika to lead a discussion. The situation I chose was fairly simple. It was one of those days, around the sixth week, when I needed to meet separately with the first of the subteams that were planning a lesson to teach to their groups. Either I can excuse the rest of the students for the last half hour of class or I can ask one of them to take my place as discussion leader.

Looking around for someone to take my place, it occurred to me that this would be a chance for Erika to express her outspokenness in the role of a teacher. I had no doubt about her confidence, and when I asked her, she said okay without hesitating. We had been talking about problems, and successes, in their field experiences, and I told the class that Erika would continue leading the discussion while I met with the planning groups.

What happened wasn't so simple. When I came back fifteen minutes later to check on their progress, Erika and Lori B. were fuming. Because I was in a hurry to get back to the planning groups, I smoothed the issue. I listened to both sides briefly and showed (read, "told") them how they have common goals. "It shouldn't be hard," I said, "to continue the discussion if you pay attention to your mutual concern for understanding the relationship of theory and practice." In that busy moment, I imagined that I'd done my job.

One more even briefer visit to the group assured me that I was wrong. Nobody had gotten up and left in the middle, but mostly people were talking in small clusters. Ten minutes later, class was over. As the students were leaving, it was obvious that I needed to hear Erika's and Lori's sides of the story. When I talked with the two of them outside of class, Erika complained that Lori had been making distracting comments. Lori didn't disagree. This was her normal behavior, she said, and I didn't disagree. Her comments never bothered me, though, and when I had wanted more of her attention, I quietly told her so. She complained that Erika called on her and said that, as she wasn't interested in the discussion, what would she like the group to talk about? Lori said she didn't know. It must have been about then that I had visited the group the first time.

The conflict cooled after each had been heard. It didn't become a big class issue, and for most I think it was just something that normally happens in a classroom—which is true. What was left over were some people who were annoyed with Erika's confrontational nature and some who were pleased that she had called Lori on her behavior. Until writing this story, it didn't occur to me that I might have used their conflict as a problem for the class to think about. Then again, I think I was smarter just to let sleeping dogs lie. It wasn't the most congenial class I ever taught, but as the story of the four panels unfolded, we all learned more about expressing our voices and listening to each other.

During the week and a half that we were planning the panels, Erika was among the majority who complained that they didn't know what they were supposed to do. She didn't exhibit her usual confidence. I don't think she was nervous about the task though. A better description is feisty, which characterized most of the complainers. And I knew from experience that at this point in the semester students were well prepared to push on me.

In this group, of all the students it was Kenyatta who was the most nervous—

unconsoled by knowing that she was only a panelist, without a leadership role. The story she told in her final paper described the planing process as "talk soup." She caricatured the dialogue:

> "Well, what do you all want to talk about?"
> "I don't know."
> "Does anyone have any ideas?"
> "This assignment isn't fair."
> "I don't know what we are supposed to do."

Erika and Janice were responsible for leading the planning discussion. Their unsureness added to Kenyatta's primary concerns about speaking in front of the class. And when, on the day of the panel, three members didn't show up, she was truly beside herself.

~

It was a tough decision whether to go ahead with the second panel when we realized that three people in the group were missing. Erika and Janice were prepared and psyched, so we checked it out with Kenyatta and Candice. They reluctantly agreed because Erika and Janice, besides asking them questions, were willing to participate in the discussion too.

Erika was sensitive to Kenyatta and asked her to share a favorite story first. By the time the discussion turned next to Candice, she no longer seemed to mind talking in front of the class. By the end, she actually contributed as much as everyone else. Candice retold a story about Totto-chan's insistence on taking two sickly chicks home from school to care for them. They died three days later, and even though Totto-chan had been warned, she learned a hard lesson about loss and grief. It was touching to listen to Candice and Erika, and others who joined in, talking over the story, about their own experiences, and about a teacher's responsibility in a situation like this.

Next, Janice spoke about Totto-chan's experience of talking with headmaster Kobayashi for a whole morning, the story that I like so much. Oddly, when Janice finished Erika didn't pause for comments. She followed immediately with her own favorite incident—a teacher so insensitive to a student's handicap that Mr. Kobayashi was angered. Again she didn't invite any comments. Instead, dissatisfied with the results of the planning meetings, Erika had cooked up a plan of her own, which she now unleashed.

I was surprised. I suspect that others didn't notice the shift. Very matter of fact, she said, "This reminds me of two recent stories of teachers humiliating very young students. One I heard this week on a talk show, and the other I read in the newspaper. Maybe you know about them. One was about a white teacher who was upset with a black third-grade student because she always forgets her glasses. The teacher sent her home with 'Where are my glasses?' written on the child's face. The other case in the news was about a first-grade boy who kissed a girl in his class and was charged with sexual harassment. Let's start with the first problem. What do you think?"

There was a lively discussion for the rest of class. There were lots of opinions and arguments and a real boost of excitement. Unfortunately, it was the kind of discussion that I so strongly believe doesn't go anywhere. Interrupting is the norm, and the focus changes rapidly with little opportunity to pursue a line of thinking or feeling. Sometimes a student does take the discussion back to an earlier junction, but it never stays there long. I listened attentively, as I had promised myself, but I didn't say anything.

In some ways, I knew then what had happened. These kinds of panel discussions were typical in previous semesters, before I had decided to insist on a tighter structure that I hoped would lead to more of what I wanted. It occurred to me that I might have gone too far. My plans left too little room for my students to express their personal energy. I was not unaware that the first panel and the beginning of the second were certainly less enthusiastic than usual.

Since then, I've read Erika's version of what happened. "Five days before our presentation, our group did a practice discussion. At first, the discussion was virtually nonexistent because of my approach. I tried to stick exactly to what was written in the 'Panel Notes.' This proved to be boring. The group wasn't interested in talking about the books. I was discouraged by this. I didn't like how my success as a moderator was riding on someone else's participation. Our boat was sinking. I decided to suggest that we take universal, interesting topics and relate them to the books, and everyone agreed. By the end of our practice run, I felt confident again."

From this, her plan developed. She further wrote, "In Janice's wrap-up, after thanking everyone for their participation, she pointed out how we really did agree that there are limits to a teacher's freedom and how, even though we argued a lot, this is something we have to think about. I was very proud of our group. We did really well. As a matter of fact, I think we did better than all the other groups. In conclusion, leading the panel was a good example of freedom in the classroom. We were given guidelines, yet we were able to determine the outcome of the discussion. We were free to guide the conversation however we wanted. In spite of my earlier complaints, I enjoyed leading my first panel discussion." Then, I could empathize with how the panel turned out for her. At the time, though, my gut reaction was displeasure.

In contrast, the student reactions were mostly positive. In the last five minutes before I dismissed class, I asked what people liked about today's panels, and I referred to the two topics that Erika introduced as tangents. Candice didn't take me to task then, but she was clear enough in her journal: "It seems that I'm not so articulate about my views in front of a large group as I am in a small group. I was a little uncomfortable up there, but it went okay. I'm glad Erica overcame her dislike of the assignment and was able to do it. I didn't think the topics from the talk show and newspaper were tangents. The themes of racism and sexism are very important. I think we needed to talk about them."

I never doubted the importance of these topics, but I strongly felt that, if we were going to talk about them, we had to find ways to listen to each other better.

THIRD PANEL

Moderator: Jessica
Side Person: Kenyatta C.
Wrap-Up: Shannon
Panel Members: Carolyn, Mark, and Bernadette

Wednesday morning began with a surprise. The minute I walked into class, Erika came over and told me that her mother, who was obviously sitting across the room, had come into town Tuesday evening and decided to spend the next two days going to classes with her daughter. "Is it all right for her to visit?" she wanted to know. For a second I thought, Is she as feisty as her daughter? Audibly, I said, "Of course."

Normally, I am open to and interested in having visitors in my classes. An experience a few weeks ago with Erika, though, brought up a red flag. She had voiced an opinion in her group in a way that seemed to me to be almost a racial slur, and, for sure, it was insensitive. I discussed the remark with her, and she said that her mother had taught her to stand up as an African American for what she believed. This I supported. But, I added, how and when we say things make a difference. We ended up with empathy for each other's concerns, but memories of this interchange caused me to hesitate.

On the sunnier side, I was aware that Lori B., following this presentation, would moderate the last panel. It pleased me that she and Erika, who came head to head earlier in the semester, would have a chance to compare their leadership styles. There was even a chance that their conflict might be addressed.

~

We got the third panel going without a hitch. At the time, my feelings were still confused: I liked the higher energy of the second panel, and yet I was unwilling to give up pushing students to hear each other fully. Six vignettes further un-cover pieces of the puzzle.

Leaders

Jessica didn't stand out in my mind. She was a good student who did her work and, sometimes, participated in class discussions. Nothing wrong with that, I just didn't know any more about her. Maybe because of this, I didn't expect her to be a moderator.

From her final paper, I learned that she was more prepared than I realized.

Waiting till Wednesday was useful to her. She wanted to get ideas from the first two panels. It became clear to her that as a moderator you have to balance everything. You have to be a good listener, and you have to keep the discussion flowing in the right direction. You have to maintain control, but at the same time, you can't be too strict. Everyone's interest is important, and yet there is a need to stay focused on what you are trying to present. For Jessica, a synonym for *moderator* was *teacher*, and she recognized that this was my intent. I was impressed.

On the day of the panel discussion, after it had been going along for a while, she noticed that Kevin and Lori B. were having a conversation of their own. It made her mad. She thought for a few moments about how to remedy the situation without embarrassing anyone. She decided to ask Kevin if there was a question or comment that he wanted to address to the panel, adding that this was the time for everyone in the audience to get involved. From Kevin's defensive response, it was obvious to her that he felt singled out.

His comparison, though, of children's attention span to that of puppies did bring attention to him—and his back to the class. He got a big laugh. Knowing that he had a serious side, she encouraged him to explain. There was an energetic debate. It came to an end when she added that even adults can sometimes have the attention span of puppies. This time she got a laugh. She regretted insinuating that he should pay more attention to his own restlessness. She didn't want to embarrass him further. It worked out, though, because the discussion got back on track.

Kenyatta C., a serious young man, brought to everything in his life a religious spirit. On the day of the panel, he also had a lot of butterflies. Part of him wished he were the moderator because then he would have more control over the conversation. The job of the side person seemed harder to him. Then he decided that this was an even better way to overcome his fear of public speaking. His reading had reminded him of the importance of not setting limits on what one can do. This was going to be a greater challenge, and he liked that.

From his view, the panel discussion was about the development of the teacher self. It made everyone focus inwardly and ask difficult questions about how a successful, caring teacher should behave. It required asking what it means to become a teacher who is expressing his or her own personality. What the panel didn't cover for him was the role of moral education in today's classrooms. In his practicum, he had realized that many of the children were missing inner discipline and a knowledge of good and bad that is so important. Kenyatta felt strongly that schools needed more structure.

Shannon, on several occasions, was ready to add her thoughts to the discussion, but because the panel was going so well, getting a word in edgewise didn't seem to be worth the effort. Besides, her task was to do the wrap-up, and Jessica and

Kenyatta weren't looking for her to take a turn. She kept herself busy taking notes while everyone else was talking.

When Jessica finally turned to her, announcing that the panel discussion was over, Shannon wanted to give a short speech. Because of the time, she only thanked the audience and added, "By sharing our views on various issues, we hope we have given everyone new ideas to think about. We hope they will expand the thoughts you came with today."

Later I learned what she wanted to say. She wrote, "Freedom in the classroom proved to be an excellent topic for us to discuss. It was easy to talk about our readings and relate them to practical experience. I learned how important it is to develop a good teacher-student relationship. If students don't trust or respect the teacher, their ability to learn will be affected. At the same time, the teacher must consider the children's feelings and know not to overstep their boundaries. Mutual respect is the goal.

"Teachers need to have confidence in themselves and their students. A negative attitude will affect both the teacher's ability to teach a lesson and the students' ability to learn it. This means that a teacher must have control over the class without being too forceful. Acting the role of a strict authoritarian scares students, and this makes students feel that they don't have any freedom.

"There are many ways in which the teacher self can be developed. I hope that one day I will become an effective, understanding teacher who will be able to get through to my students without overstepping my boundaries or theirs. I don't want to violate the freedom that helps students learn."

Panelists

I discovered in the first few weeks of class that Carolyn had teacher intuitions that were similar to mine. I don't tend to favor one student over another, but I have to admit that I often looked to her for help when other students were confused. One student's explanation to another is far better than my repeating myself. At the conclusion of a week's work, I could count on her for a helpful summary. My commitment to understanding all the students whenever they spoke was no less. My tendency to nod agreement to her without having to clarify what she was saying, though, certainly was greater.

In contrast, Carolyn was absent too many times and was often late. I was understanding because she had a dream about becoming a teacher. Her two children, though not finished with high school, were old enough to care for many of their own needs. And they believed in her dream too. She felt new life when she was accepted at the university. Still, after so many years, academic learning was unfamiliar, the children couldn't go without some attention; furthermore, she had to work full-time. It was hard, and there were times when one thing or another had to give. I was disappointed that she couldn't give more attention to class, but she did do all the assigned work and participated fully when she was present. Besides, she knew so much already. I wasn't worried.

The bigger stumbling block was her lack of confidence. She was plagued with self-doubt. But her persistence, a kind of useful stubbornness, kept her going. Of great help to her were the opportunities to speak out about what she already knew of teaching—what she was sure about. On the panel today, when no one else was talking, she was ready at every moment to add to the conversation. She felt she had so much to say. Later, Carolyn was joyous when she learned that she was quoted in Chari's final paper.

"The individual who stood out the most on the third panel was Carolyn. She always provides me with food for thought and greatly helps me tap into my inner self. One thing she said that day I remember exactly: 'To learn, there is a knowledge wheel within us that needs to be guided. It can't spin rapidly without structure. Every student has a natural desire and interest in learning. The teacher's main goal should be to spark this desire and interest.' "

The second panelist was Mark. He busied himself thinking about what others were saying but often stayed quiet because, even when he was ready with his own opinion, he didn't like to interrupt. That's how it was today when Carolyn, late, finally settled into her chair on the panel. Jessica was moving the discussion from the books to a more general question. "First, I'd like to get an opinion from our panel of what they think freedom in the classroom entails."

When Mark and Bernadette hesitated, Carolyn jumped at the chance. She talked about children needing space, letting them explore their creative energies, problems that will come up, and ways to handle the problems. Her answer was long, and, for Mark, what she said was true and not so new. Much of this had been covered by the other panels already. Mark felt that there was nothing to add. Afterward, Jessica questioned him. He said that he didn't have anymore to say, and Bernadette nodded agreement. Carolyn helped Jessica out by adding a few thoughts to her own.

Kenyatta shifted the conversation, "So Mark, where do you stand when it comes to discipline in the classroom?" The question to him was not surprising. He and Kenyatta had discussed it when preparing for the panel the week before. In his "Panel Notes," Mark had written, "Would I be able to run a classroom like the one in *Totto-chan* without resulting in total chaos?" They disagreed. Kenyatta felt that the ideas in *Totto-chan* were impractical. Mark wasn't sure, but he knew he didn't intend to be a strict disciplinarian. He was concerned about embarrassing a student.

Mark spoke about a child with whom he was having some difficulty. Other school experiences were brought up. Two examples showed how teachers managed to keep control without being heavy-handed. The discussion grew livelier, and the audience got into it too.

Bernadette was pleased with the leadership that Mark and Leah (absent today) provided when they were teaching her group last week about the emotional side of learning. It was her observation that they had good control of the discussion. They kept it focused. She had been wary of working in small groups all semester and was pleased to have this experience. It bothered her greatly whenever people talked incessantly and seemed to add so little. I assumed that she was shy, but she saw herself as withdrawn only when the discussion wasn't meaningful to her.

She felt that the idea of the panels was good at first because many interesting points were covered while they were preparing. By the time it came to do the discussion in front of the whole class, though, her feelings had changed. What soured her began with Erika's panel. Yes, the issues were relevant to education, but it wasn't what they were supposed to be discussing. Instead of talking about freedom to learn, the conversation had strayed. It was too much like a talk show where so little listening takes place. Today, her positive attitude gave way completely when Carolyn, arriving late, proceeded to give long speeches and no one tried to limit how much she spoke. She participated very little and only when pressed.

Bernadette was discouraged, and this made her sad and upset. In her final paper, which was more a letter to me, she apologized for being absent the last two weeks of class. The fear of having to explain her feelings kept her away. It was too soon to explain.

~

Throughout the progress of the third panel, I was least aware of Bernadette's feelings and hardly conscious of the other undercurrents that were taking place. Had I known, my underlying ambivalence surely would have been heightened. By the time the fourth panel was ready to go, though, the class mood, including mine, was simply good.

I also had stopped thinking about Erika's mom. She had been listening attentively to this opening panel and was only a vague worry by now. At this point, a relevant question or a brief remark from her would have been welcome because I feel that a visitor's understanding is heightened by being involved. I do like having visitors. What I don't like is someone overshadowing the students and what I want the class to accomplish.

FOURTH PANEL

Moderator: Lori B.
Side Person and Wrap-Up: Kevin
Panel Members: Steve, Jamie L., and Kristen

Least resistant of all the panel leaders, Lori was a bit confused at first but soon took on the task of preparing for her role with interested anticipation. Displaying her worries about holding out for thirty minutes, her notebook was filled with questions from the "Panel Notes," ideas from the books, and comments that she had heard in their planning discussions the week before. With these in hand, she was surer of guiding her group successfully. It seemed to her that whenever everyone could share how they think and feel, she got the best learning experience possible. Now, this was a special opportunity for the group to shine. I may have influenced this thought by asking them to go last because, I said, their group was the most energetic.

Lori asked Kevin to introduce the panel. She wasn't abdicating her role as moderator. She thought it would be more lively to begin with his quirky antics. Different than Josh, whose antics were mostly in how he moved, Kevin's were with words. These were what established his claim to being another class character. I was surprised by the switch but trusting. After his introduction, she calmly guided questions and answers.

My only concern, and mild at that, was for Kristen. When class met in a large group, it was rare for her to say anything. This challenge was meant for everyone in class, and still, I didn't want any student to be unduly embarrassed. It wasn't a problem. Kristen, though speaking quietly, had something important to her to say. I particularly liked her comment, "Freedom in the classroom means more than letting students off the hook or letting them run wild. It means allowing them to make decisions and voice their opinions. The teacher should be kind enough to listen to these opinions yet firm enough to keep students' respect and accomplish the lessons. I realize that this makes teaching a difficult career."

For a short while, though, the discussion did seem to be repeating what had been said on the other panels. Even without seeing into the thoughts of the members of the third panel, the doubts that had arisen on Monday reappeared. What I was hearing, in fact, again sounded much like "freedom *or* structure," as it had on Monday. The repeat performance didn't last long.

Steve made a target of himself, and the other panel members took him on. Based on his school experience, he argued that a military style of education had importance. His only give was that this would be true until you became an adult—vaguely recognizing that what we had been talking about in class all semester didn't fit his model, not at all recognizing that military education is designed for adults. He chose words that drew confrontation: "I think a classroom can only be successful if the teacher is elusive, stern, and has complete control." With the perspective of time, he himself wrote, "I realized that I was virtually unbending in my view of freedom in the classroom."

Members of the audience were now waving their hands trying to get Lori's attention. One of them, five seats to my right, was Erika's mother. Actually, she wasn't waving her hand, it was just politely raised, and her eyes weren't directed toward the moderator, she was looking at me. In the pause of someone's breath, she said, "Can I say something?" The tension I felt was mainly connected with someone addressing me. I didn't consider myself in charge because I was a member of the audience. My answer was predictable, "It's up to Lori to call on people."

Lori, of course, called on Erika's mother. She pointed out that freedom and discipline were not opposites. Her tone, though, was gently reprimanding, and I think this is what catalyzed, as Steve noted later, the start of an exhilarating discussion. Bolstered by arguments from Kristen and Lori, Jamie forcefully defended the panel: "This is exactly what we are saying. I believe that freedom in the classroom means structured open discussion, letting the children share in the direction of the learning. I believe that people are distorting the real meaning of freedom."

Atypically, Kevin was quiet. Lori noticed and called on him. "I was thinking," he said. "I was taught nothing in this course, yet I learned more than I had in any other course."

Now the panel and the audience were up in arms again—defending me. All they seemed to have heard was "taught nothing." The heat of the discussion was palpable. Comments came from every direction. A few even sounded angry with Kevin. One might say that Lori was inviting members of the audience to participate, but really their clamoring for turns to speak gave her no choice. Though people were still talking one at a time, the discussion was pretty much out of control.

I knew that the panel discussions had accomplished what I wanted. I also knew, because no one was checking a wristwatch, that shortening the fourth panel a few minutes would be unnoticeable. I decided it would be more helpful to use the remaining time for reactions to our week's work, and I gave Lori the five-minutes-left signal. Kevin's wrap-up was more a continuation, though at a lower pitch, and so by the time he announced that time had completely run out, the compelling need to speak had subsided.

A few students shared their reactions, and they were consistent with mine. The panel discussions turned out to be fun, and, Kevin's opinion notwithstanding, the teachers, that is, the moderators and their helpers, did play an important role in our learning. It would have been nice to have also heard Steve say what he later wrote: "Not until the discussion was over did I realize that I had debunked freedom in front of the whole class. It's ironic. While I am arguing that this kind of teaching can never be successful, I enjoy being in a classroom where I have the freedom to say so." I didn't miss it, though, because the feeling of irony was in the air.

"Before we end, is there anyone else who wants to add something?" Erika's mother raised her hand, and I nodded. Addressing the panel, she said, "This comment might sound coarse . . . but . . .

[Red flag/what will happen next is going to mess up a great class/this is not the place for heavy criticism/speak to me after class about a problem, and I'll take time on the Monday coming up for a discussion/we'll have time to deal with it/we have all worked hard and deserve to be appreciated for our efforts/with this as a basis, it is then possible to hear and respond meaningfully to what needs to be changed/but Not Now!

Of course, I thought none of this in the microsecond that exists between two spoken words. I have been teaching long enough, however, to feel all of them in that instant.]

. . . I want to say that when I write a big fat check every semester for Erika's tuition, I always wonder whether the education she is getting is worth it. And now I know. What happened in class today is what education is all about."

I was so touched. I thanked her, and then I was embarrassed. I mumbled something, probably not understandable to anyone expect those close to me, about how it is all of us together who make this happen. A voice inside said, "Take it in, she's giving you a high compliment." And I did. It was a wonderful note on which to end.

Bernadette's feelings are still a quandary. I like to believe that when a class is this good, it works for everyone. Life's not like that though. Still, the structure helped us achieve the freedom we desired.

11

The Artist and the Gardener

Another course I teach is a graduate version of the undergraduate "Art and Science of Teaching" class. Although the focus is slanted to fit the needs of experienced teachers, I discovered that graduate students were interested in the same books and classroom group activities as the undergraduates.

For the last class activity, in both courses, I ask the students to draw what they have learned over the semester. The pictures are brought to class the final week, and they are posted on the board as the center for a lengthy discussion. Two graduate students, my daughter Rachel, who teaches photography, and Jennifer, who is an elementary school teacher, describe the thoughts, feelings, and experiences behind their drawings. I have woven their two stories into one.

With the term nearly over, Rachel was enjoying sitting in a circle with her classmates listening to her father talk about the final paper. At first, it was strange being in his class. It was a small graduate class, though, only ten students, and they got to know and like each other quickly. The group members had fun working together. The strange feeling disappeared when Rachel realized that no one else was paying attention to their special relationship. Because no one called him Professor Allender, she even got used to calling her father Jerry.

At this moment, though, there was also a tension in class that comes from hearing about homework. "However," Jerry said, "you don't have to do the last of the experience experiments, three are enough." There was a group sigh, and a few, "Oh good"s, to which he responded, "Please keep in mind the value of experience experiments. I myself continue to do them regularly. Besides trying out new ideas, they are a helpful way to reflect on the practice of teaching."

Rachel nodded in agreement, yet, in spite of herself, she heard a small voice inside singing, "Less homework, yeah, less homework, yeah, less homewo—."

The song stopped midword, as Jerry said, "There is one other final assignment. Instead of the fourth experience experiment, I want you to use the time off over Thanksgiving to draw, covering the whole semester, what you have learned about creating an effective learning environment."

Rachel responded with others, out loud, almost in chorus, "Draw???"

"Yes," he said, "we will share and discuss the drawings during the final week of class. If you are uncomfortable with drawing, you can do a collage or some other creative alternative. It's also okay to use some words if necessary, but make the main focus visual. We're going to hang the pictures on the blackboard, so be sure they are big enough to see from where we sit."

There was an air of hesitation. He seemed to expect the resistance because it didn't phase him. He went on to talk about the value that this task has had for other students. Finally he said, "You'll do what you do," which has been his way of indicating that he is open to individual interpretations of his assignments. Knowing her father, Rachel knew too that he was confident that everyone would bring in a picture of their learning after Thanksgiving.

The class discussion moved on, but Rachel's mind remained on the drawing. She realized that, given the nature of the course, the assignment made sense. Thinking back to the weeks they had spent exploring the importance of visual learning, imagery, and multiple intelligences, she could have expected the assignment.

But drawing was something she had not done for a long time. Drawing for a class, even a comfortable class like this one, felt uncomfortable. So much of her adult life had been shaped by a belief in her inability to draw. In her undergraduate days, she registered for courses in photography and laughingly told her friends that she took them because she couldn't draw. Later, after being accepted in an art school for graduate studies in photography, she told people that she was probably the only art student ever accepted who couldn't even draw an acceptable stick figure. It was a funny joke at parties, but underneath there was a confused bundle of feelings.

Reminiscing, there had been many art classes in elementary school and even some in high school. More than that, she recalled a burlap bag of art supplies among the things in her bedroom from when she was quite small. The supplies had been a birthday gift, she was sure, from her parents. In her mind's eye, she could clearly see them resting on the bottom shelf of the bookcase in that childhood bedroom.

It wasn't long, though, before the assignment got lost in the excitement over the panel discussion that was being presented by five of her classmates. When she got home, there was Sasha wagging his tail looking for attention, the answering machine with its blinking light, and the interrupted discussion with Eric over breakfast about plans for Thanksgiving. She made a note to schedule time for the assignment and put it out of her mind.

It was the beginning of spring, and the gardener deep in thought walked until she came to an empty plot of land. She looked around, and only then did she realize how far she had walked. She could see none of the rooftops of the village from where she had come. It was from there that she had received the pouch around her neck. She had been given a pouch of assorted seeds. "Care for these seeds," she was told, "for we have no more land on which to plant them." The people were tearful, but when they saw the gardener's wheelbarrow filled with tools, they smiled. The gardener carefully took the pouch in both hands, and she smiled too.

The gardener had been accustomed to caring for indoor plants. Indoor plants came with tags that told of their names, how best to grow them and in what kind of soil, how much light and how much water, and whether or not they required fertilizer. The seeds carried in the pouch had no instructions. The gardener didn't even know their names. She peeked inside the pouch and, in a moment of panic, said to herself, "Perhaps, I'll keep them all together inside the pouch. Certainly, less harm will come to them that way. Yes, it's better for the seeds to be in there." She closed the pouch.

As the gardener was imagining the seeds nestled together within the pouch held in her hands, she felt an unevenness that she had not felt before. She sat down, opened the pouch again, and carefully poured the seeds out onto her flattened apron. The gardener was immediately fascinated. She saw all shapes, sizes, textures, and colors. All of them seeds, yet each one different from the others. She noticed that some of the seeds were chipped and . . . could it be? Yes, some had already sprouted. The seed coats had been pushed open by small green arms. These sprouted ones must have been the protrusions that prompted her to re-open the pouch. It was as if they were trying to tell her, "Take us out, let us grow." What about the others? she wondered. Do they want to grow too? Her heart nearly shattered at the thought of keeping these seeds trapped inside. How could she deny them the opportunity to grow, especially if that was their natural inclination?

The gardener tilled an area of dirt. She removed the debris and the stones that were there. She broke apart the big clumps of dirt with her pick and sifted a large area of land with her other tools. This was the first time she had ever used these tools, and the awkwardness of holding them formed blisters on her hands. Though they caused discomfort, she didn't stop, for her seeds needed planting. Anyway, the roughened skin would protect her from future blisters.

When the time seemed right, she gingerly poked most of the seeds into the prepared soil and sprinkled some water from her canteen over them. The ones she did not put in the ground, she planted in a small pot she had in her wheelbarrow. These seeds were the ones that looked chipped. They did not seem quite as ready as the others, and the gardener decided not to plant them with the others until they had pushed themselves upward through the soil in the pot. Before she sat down to rest, she outlined a sketch of her newly planted garden and wrote down descriptions of the seeds and where she had placed them.

While the gardener rested, she looked at all that she had done. She was happy because she felt that she had put the seeds where they wanted to be. She was excited because she couldn't wait to see what kinds of plants the seeds would grow into. But most of all, the gardener felt scared. She wanted the best for these seeds and wondered if she knew enough to help them be their best. Only one thing she knew for certain: It would be more difficult caring for the seeds now that they were out of the pouch.

Later in the evening, Rachel's thoughts turned back to the burlap bag. Mind you, not to the drawing assignment. Rather, what happened to those art supplies? Were they thrown out when she grew older or when she moved away? Her picture of them was pristine, as if they had been carefully and lovingly preserved but never used. There were other things that would have gone along with that bag. Did she still have any of them? Without answers, deeper, more troubling thoughts appeared.

Rachel has been grappling with her stalled career as an artist. Out of graduate school and into planning a do-it-yourself wedding, which was a grand creative event, she had spent more than three years not getting a new art project in the air. From her graduate school teachers, she thought she had learned how to overcome resistance. After the wedding, though, she worried more about money and less about art. She found opportunities to teach photography as an adjunct professor and, on the surface, was satisfied. After a couple of years, she got an interesting offer from a colleague to work on producing an educational TV series. She jumped at the chance, and settling into the new job seemed enough to do.

Out of the blue, the program changed—suddenly leaving her without a job. What an opportunity! Now she had the time to be an artist. The problem was that nothing happened. A few months ago, bordering on hopeless, yet always inventive, she made two small decisions. First, because she had the time, as a step toward bringing herself back to teaching she would take her father's class. And second, she decided to follow a self-help program for artists in a book that she had stumbled on.

Julie Cameron says in *The Artist's Way* that her program is for artists who feel blocked. One ongoing and difficult assignment in the book is to take weekly "artist's dates." This is playful time to explore childlike urges that are connected with creativity. A date is any activity that feels fun and is done alone. The first week, Rachel went to a film screening. It seemed as if every professional friend she had was there. It was awful. The next week she went off to a favorite coffee shop only to discover that she had left the house without any money. And as the weeks went on, her dates did not improve. For the most part, they had been a disaster.

Thus, the gardener's labor of love began, and the gardener learned how to learn from the seedlings. They were not able to change their situation themselves, but they were able to inform the gardener of what they needed. Through careful observation, the gardener saw, though all of the seeds had the same basic needs, each one required different amounts. This became evident as the seeds developed into small plants. Depending on the gardener's treatment of them, their coloring would fade or brighten, their stems would wither or stand tall, and their leaves would wilt or extend out and upward. The gardener was determined to help these plants grow, so she adjusted each plant's environment as she saw fit according to its behavior. Sometimes she had to make a series of changes before the plant would comfortably thrive. She always worried about whether she should be experimenting with their lives, but her thoughtful problem solving seemed to work out for the best.

One morning, as the gardener was making some notes, she noticed that nothing yet had grown in several spots where she had planted. She became quite concerned over these seeds, which still remained seeds while the other plants stood a few inches tall. She was tempted to dig them out of the ground, but she waited. She waited for what seemed like forever. Though she firmly believed that all seeds can grow, she was joyfully relieved when, one day not long after, she saw small shoots of green emerge from the soil. "It must not have been their time to grow before now," thought the gardener. "They just weren't really ready. After all, what does it matter when they grow, as long as they do?"

The gardener gleefully congratulated the new births and encouraged them to keep growing. Uh, wait. . . . The gardener consulted her first sketch of the garden and realized that two seeds still hadn't begun to peek out from the earth. She was glad she had been patient and waited for the recent plants to begin growing, but she couldn't stand by and wait for these two seeds to be frozen by the wintry weather without first breathing fresh air. What should she do?

The day after Jerry assigned the class to do a drawing, Rachel was stubbornly in search of a fun artist's date. She had come to dread the assignment, and this one seemed to start out like all the rest. Even though it was cold, and not knowing exactly why, she had decided to go downtown and wander in and out of stores. Glum, she did know that there were other times when this had been enjoyable. Finding herself in front of an art supply store, she figured she might as well go in. Walking up and down the isles was kind of fun; it certainly kept her warm, but she felt more drowsy than creative.

Then her eyes landed on something that caught her full attention. It was a small metal box with what looked like ten crayons in it. Looking around, she noticed that the aisle was full of watercolors. They weren't crayons, they were watercolors. The tin that caught her eye was among sets of many sizes, as many as fifty in a box, and you could even buy the colors individually. They were all expensive but lovely.

She continued to wander in the store but kept coming back to the watercolors. It occurred to her that while the bigger sets had more choices, the little set of ten could easily fit into her purse. "How nice," she thought, "with a small brush and a tiny pad, I could carry this around with me." It seemed delightful. Begrudging the money, she planned to mention it to Eric, and he could buy it for her as a holiday gift.

That evening, thinking back on her artist's date, even if it wasn't great, she remembered enjoyable moments. At dinner, she told Eric about the watercolors. Rachel could see that he wasn't listening. "He's too busy to be thinking about holiday shopping yet," she thought and let it go at that.

The following morning she checked her calendar. The morning of the day before the next class would be plenty of time to do the drawing assignment. She penciled it in and then decided to gather together the art supplies so she could get right to work that day. Rummaging through her art materials, she realized how little she had. Since art school, the supplies she wasn't using were sold off in yard sales. What was left were film and video gear and what she used to teach photography and one of her other interests, bookmaking. After fifteen minutes of scrounging, all she had to show were a few marking pens, in four colors and several repeats, and an old eight-by-ten notepad. She placed the paltry pile on the upper right corner of her desk. In the days that followed, every time she passed her desk and saw the little pile, she felt sad.

~

Much woe to the gardener. She still did not know what to do with the two lonely seeds that had never sprouted. The gardener looked over the plants that were showering the land with their beauty. They were so busy growing, they could not tell her what to do. They, in fact, seemed not to care, for they could not understand why any plant would remain inside its seed coat instead of breathing the outside air. Nothing was better than swaying in the afternoon's breezes! "Oh, of course they cannot help me," the gardener thought, "they have too many new things to experience." And certainly, she knew, it was not their priority to concern themselves over her concerns.

The tearful gardener stooped down and leaned her back against her wheelbarrow. She clutched the empty pouch around her neck and remembered when she first arrived in this place. She remembered the protrusions within the pouch she now held close to her heart. They were so ready to grow that they couldn't even wait to be planted in soil! But the other seeds did require soil, including the chipped seeds she had planted in a pot for extra care. "Oh," she thought, "perhaps these two seeds that looked fine on the outside required more."

Immediately, the gardener stood and walked over to the spot where the two seeds were planted and uncovered them. They looked exactly as they had when she took them from the pouch—their seed coats tightly wrapped around their contents. "Little seeds," the gardener said, "I'm sorry. The ground is awfully deep and does seem to go on forever in all directions. Changing and growing can be scary. Please forgive me and please let me help you not to be scared of sharing with us the beauty within you." The gardener followed the voice of her heart and placed these two seeds in a shallow container, watered them, and then loosely covered the container with a patch from her apron. She then told the seeds that they could start growing and that later, if they wanted to, they could be planted in the garden with the other plants. It wasn't long afterward that the gardener removed the cloth from the container and discovered the sweet fragrance of alyssum—for the world to enjoy.

～

Preparing to shop for Thanksgiving, Rachel recognized that she would have to squeeze in her artist's date during the three weekdays before the holiday began. Struggling again with what to do with herself for a couple of hours, she remembered the little set of watercolors. A surge of excitement ran through her. For sure, she realized, this was the feeling that an artist's date should elicit. She was enthusiastic and instantly knew why. On the Wednesday before Thanksgiving, she took a bus into town, went straight back to the art supply store, and bought a little set of supplies—the tin of ten colors, one medium-size brush, and a tiny sketch pad. From the store she headed directly to her favorite coffee shop, found a table by a window, and ordered hot cocoa and a glass full of water. When the water came, she set to work.

Rachel began by staring at the crayon-like sticks of watercolors. They were pristine, as were her memories of the burlap bag. She played with the brush and tested the colors. Then she started to fill the pages of the sketch pad with abstract images and daffodils. Her favorite flower. Page after page. Some were full of color, and some were just lines. As she painted, the set got messy, and she thought about the burlap bag. The contrast. Here, with the mixing and muddling of colors and the messy painting, this was just plain fun. She didn't want to stop. Time passed quickly, and later, looking at her watch for the first time, she didn't know when she would want to stop. This was a first for an artist's date. But Sasha needed his walk, so she cleaned up, paid for the cocoa, and headed home.

On the bus, she looked over the two hours of work. She counted five pictures of daffodils. It was no surprise. Her one-and-only doodle, for years, had been daffodils. And then it dawned on her, she had in fact used her childhood paints—to draw endless pages of daffodils. Where were those pages today? Among what she had saved? She didn't know, and it really didn't matter. Those daffodils, and the ones she had drawn today, were hardly remarkable, and that too was beside the point. What mattered was the pleasure she found in painting them and the giddy joy of the messy tin of watercolors.

She smiled to herself remembering what she had learned in graduate school. The process of art needs giddy abandon without attachment to the outcome. "That's it!" she said to herself, "I'll do dad's assignment in the same way." To draw what she had learned this semester seemed to fit with the challenge to be creative, and what's more, she looked forward to doing the assignment.

Monday morning, the day before the drawing was due, there were pressing commitments. Changing her plans at breakfast, she told Eric that dinner would be quick because she would be busy painting that evening. Monday morning, later, she managed to buy a huge piece of smooth white cardboard to use as a canvas, a little longer than three feet on one side and little less on the other.

When the time came, though, she was exhausted and without an idea of what to paint. She was disappointed but not discouraged. Troubling as it was to do homework on the day it was due, she decided she would stay home Tuesday morning until she left for class in the afternoon.

Before going to bed, to relieve the tension over still not knowing what the painting would be, she took the pens and pad that she had originally collected on her desk to try out some sketches. Doodling, symbols emerged—circles, swirls, hearts, yin-yangs—and then larger patterns of these. When a page felt wrong, she moved on to a new one. Her brief effort was interesting and fun. This was the second time in less than a week that she was enjoying her lost creativity—maybe, she grinned, it was just hiding.

Looking at the symbols and patterns, she realized that if they were arranged in a very large circle, her painting could be a mandala. It's meaning would include and go beyond the borders of the course. She liked that. From the living room, she took the big brass tray that she and Eric had received for a wedding gift, the one, sitting on a footstool, that they used as a coffee table. With a little room to spare, it fit on the cardboard. Using the tray, she could trace a huge circle. With this in mind, she went to bed.

Waking up, Rachel was excited and nervous. A clear vision of the painting was forming, but there was only one piece of cardboard. With watercolors, mistakes can't be corrected, and there was no time to start over. She remembered what one of her teachers said: "Stay with the process, and let the product take care of itself." She got up, had breakfast with Eric, cleared the dining room table as a place to work, and put on a Chopin CD.

Cautiously, with a pencil, the circle was traced and the design was blocked out. Now it was time to paint. Hesitating for a moment, she took the little brush and began. First, two yin-yangs in the center. She worked out from there. When the phone rang, she let the answering machine answer the call. When the CD ended, she quickly chose another and went right back to work. Eating lunch, and looking over her progress, she picked up the brush again while swallowing her last bite. As the hours passed, the painting grew and grew until it filled the circle and then traveled beyond to the four edges. When the whole board was filled, she set down the brush. Over the watercolors, four quotes were inked into the corners in big letters—from Gras, Rumi, Krishnamurti, and someone whose name she forgot. That one she liked the best: "If you can see the path in front of you, then it isn't yours. It's someone else's. Yours begins at the darkest place in the forest."

Summer was ending, and there was much less work for the gardener to do now. Still, she kept pursuing new ways to encourage the plants to continue growing. One afternoon, it occurred to the gardener that singing might be another way, even though she had never sung before. She opened her mouth. Hardly anything came out. She looked all around herself, and the rainbow of plants and flowers inspired her. She breathed in as much of the heavenly scents that her lungs could hold, and then she began to sing in a glorious manner, of which she never before felt herself capable. All of the creatures who had made their homes in the garden buzzed, chirped, and whirred to the gardener's tune, and the plants swayed to and fro to the rhythm of this overture to things to come.

Watching the stems, the leaves, and the blossoms dance in the breeze, the gardener too began to dance. She stretched her arms. She stretched her legs. She leaned forward and tilted back, bent to one side and then the other. She leaped into the air and whirled around the garden. She whirled and twirled and then did it again and again. The work, the blisters, the uncertainty, the self-doubt, all became worth it and complete in this moment.

Doubts appeared in Rachel's mind walking out the door headed for the bus. Maybe she hadn't done the assignment correctly. Was the painting too abstract? Was a mandala appropriate? What if it didn't make sense? What if her classmates thought she was foolish for including quotes more on the relationship of creativity and spirituality than about teaching and learning? Nearing the bus stop, a strong wind caught the cardboard canvas. She stopped thinking and concentrated on holding it tight.

For the first few moments in class, she didn't notice the other drawings. Her classmates were busy hanging their work, and she had to focus on getting her large unwieldy piece of cardboard to stay up on the blackboard. She felt better when someone, from behind her back, teased her about how big it was. Once the drawings were hung, Jerry asked the students to set up their chairs in a semicircle facing them.

For a minute, everyone sat quietly and looked. In front of them were drawings, paintings, and collages—including one collage with felt cutouts stuck on a pillowcase. There was another collage of pictures taken from magazines, and another of cutout words. An array of little sketches created a different kind of picture. There were paintings and drawings—of a bridge spanning a mountain river; a woman crossing a high wire with a balance beam; five women, or maybe it was the same woman, spinning in a circle; two dancers; and a garden. None resembled another. Not one had a clear meaning on simple inspection, but it was all impressive. "How beautiful," Rachel thought.

Rachel nudged Jennifer, who was sitting beside her, pointed to her own, and asked, "Which is yours?"

"The one with the garden in the center. The long one," she added. Jennifer's was just as high and outstretched Rachel's by another foot. It was no surprise. They had been partners for the last six weeks. Jennifer was a first-grade teacher, yet they got along well and often had similar thoughts. Compared with the others, their paintings were huge, bigger than all the rest. They laughed.

Jennifer went on, "It's my idea about students as a bag of mixed seeds that the teacher, like a gardener, has to find a way to nurture."

Rachel understood and smiled.

Greg volunteered first to stand by his work and discuss it with the class. His was drawn by a computer—symbols surrounded two dancers locked arm in arm. At the bottom, it said, "Relax, God is in charge." Rachel was relieved that someone else also had spiritual concerns. As Greg spoke, his work came alive.

When it was Rachel's turn, she stood, walked over to her painting and began, "This is where I am in my life at this moment."

Autumn was passing quickly and winter would be coming soon. The gardener was leaning against her wheelbarrow. She was thinking. Witnessing so much growth, so much life in this garden over which she had so lovingly labored, made a lump in her throat. All the plants had gotten a strong start, and there was little more she could do for them. "My dear plants and flowers," she said, "you have grown so much. Thank you for showing me that life is worth growing for. Remember how I have loved you. Believe in yourselves, always, because you have so much to offer." With these words, the gardener walked away with the empty pouch around her neck.

It was many seasons after the gardener had gone off to become a better grower of growers that she returned to her first garden. She was glad that she had left the wheelbarrow there. It was the perfect resting spot for a gardener who had traveled the world, met many other gardeners and plants of every kind, and learned new songs and dances—and even how to build special trellises and hanging baskets. Oh, yes, the gardener had learned so much, she knew she was a better grower of growers. She leaned back against her trusty wheelbarrow and quietly spoke, "My friends, show me how you've grown, and then I will sing new songs and dance new dances for you, for you have planted seeds within my heart and soul, seeds that will never stop growing."

The basic idea of a gardener honing the craft of gardening has been in my thoughts for quite some time. Ever since I read Herbert Kohl's book *Growing Minds*, I wanted to explore the notion of a teacher as a gardener planting unknown seeds. Originally, I had hoped to include all the intertwining pieces of my drawing in the story (the garden, the greenhouse, the toolshed, the well, the birdhouse, the birdbath, the picnic table, the wooden lawn chairs, the trellises, the hanging baskets, the tree, as well as a stump), but in doing so I was bogged down with too many details and explanations. I avoided this frustration by focusing on one theme, the development of the gardener's teacher self.

But in addressing this theme, I also touch on the other three themes of the course: creating an effective learning environment, the intellectual side of learning, and the emotional side of learning. A true teacher self emerges best by focusing on all of these themes in one's own learning, then consciously applying them to one's students' learning, and then back and forth. Just as my teacher self is a process of becoming, the story, I feel, will remain with me, with many revisions along my way.

—Jennifer Pakola

I continue to grapple with the nature of creativity, its role in my life, and how I define myself as an artist. I never seem to be able to shake the question, Why be an artist? It is a difficult journey that I have been on for a long time. This semester, however, it was never unclear what my dad's course had in store for me. I wanted to examine more deeply my role as a teacher. I love teaching, and I feel confident doing it. So exploring how to grow and shift within that framework always felt exciting and refreshing—even as I struggled.

Teaching is an art full of subtle nuance. Blocked as I sometimes feel as an artist, I have a very clear sense of my creativity and direction when I teach. From what I saw this semester, I have concluded that this is true for other teachers as well. Regardless of how good, or inadequate, each person felt about her- or himself as a teacher, and even if the course felt awkward for those who worked in contexts other than a classroom, no one ever questioned, "Why?" Rather, it was what and how to teach that were the questions. Teaching, complex and varied as its meanings may be, was understood to be an essential part of life.

—Rachel Allender

12

Gestalt Theory for Teachers

Jerome S. Allender and Donna Sclarow Allender

In the first half of the twentieth century, cognitive psychologists created Gestalt theory in response to what they thought, at the time, were limited concepts of how the human intellect functions. What was missing was the recognition that context, which they analyzed in terms of figure and ground, is fundamental for understanding how learning occurs. In the second half of the century, psychotherapists explored the theory's connections with emotional functioning. Here, the interplay of figure and ground was applied to understanding the learning that is involved in the development of self, particularly self in relationship with others. We see in this expanded concept a potential for better understanding the role of the teacher in a classroom. Our adaptation of Gestalt theory for educators focuses on the relevance of context to the development of the teacher self and teacher-student relationships.

Writing about Gestalt theory for teachers, however, was complicated. Because we were responsive to the contexts in which we worked, we kept our thinking fluid; the manner in which the theory was constantly modified discouraged us from making it explicit. We privileged the knowledge gained from teaching, and the insights we had were related more to these experiences than they were to theory. The process, over twenty-five years, left us with the conceptual problem of wresting words from where there were few.

Just as the stories from the course the "Art and Science of Teaching" are never the experience itself but, rather, a distillation from a point of view, so it is with this Gestalt theory for teachers. Scholarly ideas and the wise reflections of others have always been important, but their influence didn't supplant our intuitive judgments about successes in the classroom or the theoretical turns that were suggested by praxis. In order to best use the theory, develop it, and communicate its usefulness, we listened to our inner voices—using the study of our teaching as the strategy of choice for improving practice.

∼

Shifting awareness away from figural impediments to teaching and learning allows teachers and students to find both internal and external resources to achieve their goals.

Context is a powerful frame for talking about self and relationship. People notice first what is figural. The pleasure and the pain of our everyday experience, the successes and the mishaps, naturally capture our attention. The ability, though, to learn from our experiences, to reshape and expand the possibilities, is primarily dependent on our understanding of the background within which figural events take place. These starting points, figure and ground, are essential to the development of Gestalt theory. We used them to understand the context of teaching and learning.

Students have a strong tendency to feel blocked by conflicts that confront them in the classroom. This is likely to happen when students' needs and values are disregarded by the teacher, often leading to their sense of failure. Because the conflicts are figural, they appear insurmountable. But in the ground in which this figure is set, there is always a fuller range of experience that includes some skills associated with success. The ability to tap the sources of personal power and energy needed to resolve an impasse is aided by increasing the field of awareness. Teachers' fundamental goal of broadening awareness can also be used to enlarge the understanding of the learner's self. Thus, inner resources as well as those in the environment can be recognized and made available.

However, identifying students' prior successes is not enough. The memory of personal successes is often overshadowed by the memory of failed efforts—particularly when there are feelings of humiliation. Some of these experiences continue to be painful. The unconscious memory of this pain constricts the willingness to risk exploring the environment more widely because there is a fear of restimulating the injurious experience. Unfortunately, students typically accumulate a body of educational abuse. These cumulative memories build significant impediments to learning.

The impediments may seem to be largely a psychotherapeutic issue. In large measure, it is not appropriate for a teacher to take the role of a therapist, but neither can a teacher responsibly ignore these learning blocks. A practical approach is to broaden the field of the learning task to make room for relevant positive memories to surface. Remembered strengths offer more options for both the student and the teacher. For example, a child who is habitually stumbling over arithmetic will have a better chance of learning when a teacher finds out about earlier successes, no matter how small, and builds on them. This information is used to adjust the assignment, thereby bringing it, with newfound interest, within reach of the student.

No less for teachers. In the preceding stories, the teacher and students alike modified assignments to finesse fears and draw on abilities for which there is intrinsic confidence. Tracy's fear of the children in an inner-city school, in chapter 3, "Experience Experiments," is reduced by giving her some say over her field placement. Jerry's awareness of Shawn's humiliation in chapter 6, "Human Dominoes," pressures him to redesign how small groups are formed. In chapter 11, "The Artist and the Gardener," the teacher provides tacit approval for Rachel and Jennifer to adapt the final drawing assignment to meet their needs. From the first story to the last, obstacles confronting the teacher and the students must be overcome by shifting the figure in the ground.

The full educational meaning of context includes teachers, students, administrators, parents, and everyone else in the community who has a stake in what schools are supposed to accomplish. Students have goals, as do teachers, and though they may overlap, they are never totally the same. So it is with the other stakeholders. The goals of education can range from self-fulfillment to maintaining a class society assuring more benefits for some. Better understanding of the larger context of teaching reveals complexities that are often problematic, but consciousness of them allows the teacher to work toward resolutions more effectively.

These different views impinge on the learning abilities of each student. Each stakeholder brings pressures to the classroom that cannot be ignored, and these divergent pressures are a part of the learning context. The teacher's answer to the multiplicity of pressures lies in keeping the classroom environment as flexible and open-ended as possible. For this, it is necessary to have mutually responsive relationships that are lively and vital between the teacher and the students and among the students. Under these conditions, we believe that the movement between figure and ground is optimized.

Joining intellectual, emotional, and body awareness assures the development of a teacher self that supports interactive relationships in the classroom.

From years of experience growing up in school, ideas about how teachers are supposed to behave often reflect a very rigid classroom. There is a lack of adequate role models for learning how to build interactive educative relationships. A child's early school experiences not only define a student self, they also begin to create an image of a teacher self. This image continues to develop throughout life even absent the intention of ever teaching. In children's play and in normal social discourse, it is common for the teacher self to appear when conversation turns to a topic that connects with a personal competence. What we usually see is the "teacher" telling others what they should know—with little room for discussion.

Even after many years of teaching, no one is immune from making this mistake—and a mistake it is if we aim toward a more effective learning environment. It is necessary to modify this image if a teacher chooses to be more flexible and open-ended. To begin with, the tendency in all of us to tell students answers must be acknowledged. Beyond this, it should be recognized that the development of the teacher self is complex and that our concerns change as we gain experience. Teachers must engage in continuous self-study to heighten their awareness. With this approach, teachers might be more comfortable or even eager to experiment with untried behaviors.

There is a poignant story of a student teacher from one of the classes who was tutoring four young boys in a reading group. Frustrated with constant misbehavior, she was hell-bent on keeping a tight rein on them. From her own report, her relationship with them was unusually tense, and she was disturbed by her ineffectiveness. In a discussion, the class probed some of the details of the lesson and some of the larger context. It turned out she had a son the same age as these boys who was having great difficulty learning to read. The tension was over making sure that the same difficulties didn't happen again here. Her mind was concentrating on her son's failure and her own for not being able to help him. Little attention was paid to the individual problems that each of these four boys presented.

It wasn't difficult to establish that her fear of failing, unrealistically heightened by memories of trying to teach her son to read, clouded her general sense of confidence in the classroom. The insight helped to shift her attention—shifting the figure in the ground—to the situation actually confronting her. The class was able to talk about each of the four children in the group and what she estimated were their individual strengths and weaknesses. At this point, the teacher sensed her own strengths and found confidence for what might happen in their next meeting.

Feelings that are unexplored infect relationships. Embarrassment and the more powerful emotion of shame in connection with teachers' feelings of inadequacy are likely to cause an intolerance of students' floundering. The source can be as simple as a lack of subject matter knowledge or an absence of creative methods for teaching; it can be as complicated as an array of painful memories. The result is the same: There is little room for students to explore and discover their own answers. Open-endedness in the learning process produces too much tension and anxiety in the teacher who is insecure. Awareness of emotional issues like these allows resistance to be reduced and increases the possibilities for structuring the learning environment more interactively. Emotional awareness is a key element in the development of the teacher self.

A more thorough understanding, however, of this student teacher's insight and how the class worked together to assist her transformation also requires some attention to intellectual awareness. It played no less an important role in the discussion than did emotional awareness. Unraveling the emotional issues was aided by clearly identifying what was happening, not only for the teacher but for the four young students. There needed to be attention to the way the teacher influenced the ongoing flow of events.

What works is an intellectual process that puts experience in a new light, such as journaling, discussion, or any other means that reveal assumptions being made about what is real. Here, our collaborative discussion was most generative, and in this case there was little emphasis on analysis. Clearly describing the events, and specifying the ideas connected with these events, was most helpful. Intellectual awareness, in general, contributes to a clearer picture of emotional awareness.

Beyond recognizing that these two sources of awareness must be tapped and integrated, we advise paying attention as well to the normal tensions that are regularly experienced physically in the body. They too store helpful information that informs the teacher self. In essence, a teacher's comfort and discomfort begin with the way the body is used. Athletes, dancers, musicians, actors, and performers of all stripes know that how the body is organized for action is a key factor in high-level performance. Teachers and students, no less, have to perform, and the physical comfort that attends teaching and learning significantly enhances the ability to address challenge in the classroom.

"Sit up straight," teachers are known to say; and everyone in class changes his or her position. But we have seen that when this is followed by, "Now, sit comfortably," everyone changes position again. What is this about? Teachers certainly know that reading the body language of students tells a lot about their degree of involvement, and the teacher's body tells a similar story. Brief exercises for noticing tensions in the body and finding comfort in posture and movement, in fact, increase awareness on all levels. It happens, for example, that opening the chest has the effect of opening our hearts and our minds. The problems of body awareness are more complex than this, but even small beginnings can be significant.

The conscious joining of the intellect, emotions, and physical feelings offers access to intuitions that contribute to the desired development of self—here, the teacher self. Each kind of awareness is important, but joining them offers something more. From this vantage, teachers are better role models for students. Putting themselves in the position of working effectively on their own learning, they exemplify the awareness needed to succeed. What we ask of students should not be different from what we ask of ourselves; the teachers' personal empowerment best prepares them to empower students. When the intellectual, emotional, and physical all work in partnership, our inner voices are confident that we know how to learn. This is the mark of empowered people.

As teachers, our quest is to have two strong inner voices. One is needed to speak for the student self in ourselves. This is the primary source of empathy in the classroom. It allows teachers to answer the question, How would I feel if I were this student, or these students, in this situation? The other voice is that of a competent teacher. This does not mean a know-it-all. This voice reflects strengths and a willingness to admit weaknesses—it is both confident and flexible. Together, the voices of the teacher and student selves expand the possibilities for building interactive relationships in the classroom.

A lively give-and-take relationship between teacher and students requires permeable boundaries of self that provide opportunities for interpersonal contact in the here and now.

What kind of relationship do teachers want with their students? Some aim to transmit no more than specific information or a set of skills without further engagement, for example, lecturers at a university. Others want students to behave in prescribed ways without regard for the learners' wishes. Keeping still is often paramount, as are acting and responding in line with specific expectations. Many teachers too have broader goals. Like ourselves, they aim toward lively give-and-take interactions that include listening to everyone in class, paying attention to requests from all sides, and above all enjoying each other's company.

When eschewing the rigid classroom, however, teachers and students alike often form images of a learning environment where there is little or no authority left in the hands of the teacher. We are not dismissing a teacher's necessary authority or suggesting that a teacher is meant to have a peer relationship with students. Teachers are responsible to set broad goals and limits, and what happens in the classroom must be kept within these parameters except under rare circumstances. At times, students will rebel, quietly with inaction, loudly with complaints, more forcefully by blatantly misbehaving, or with some combination of all three. These interruptions must be addressed but not necessarily stifled. Our concept of leadership functions as a loose structure that permits and encourages experimentation while it maintains limits.

Balancing experimentation and limits takes a special effort. This is the same work needed to build any other interactive relationship. Therefore, it is no surprise to encounter resistance and struggle on the part of the students and the teacher. And educators have unique concerns. They have curricular pressures that limit the time available for interpersonal processes. These pressures never cease, but neither can they be overlooked.

The challenge of responding sensitively to needs and wants on all sides requires more than rigidly enacting a set of specific expectations. In a classroom where the teacher's and students' roles are played in a traditional manner, each person knows clearly what is expected. With a bit of cooperative spirit, what takes place moves along smoothly and produces a level of comfort. In the long run, though, these behaviors are not promising. Room to respond positively to deviations from the norm is left out. In contrast, when the classroom environment is less carefully defined, opportunities for finding a better fit between the teacher's and students' needs and wants are always present. However, a tolerance for ambiguity and unpredictability is necessary.

When committed to flexibility, every moment is an opportunity to try out new behaviors. This moment in Gestalt terms is the here and now. Like the issue of authority, however, it is another source of misunderstanding. If we value the here and now, how is it possible to believe in a curriculum that has been developed in the past and anticipates the future? The answer lies in a conception of "the here and now" as itself flexible. Gestalt psychologists use the concept not to limit people to a hedonistic present but to help them make choices about what from the past and the future will productively impact the present. Thus, an aware teacher chooses the present rather than being driven by unconscious fears from past experiences or concerns about what the class "should" be doing in the future. Our strategy is to find ways to make the curricular anxieties of teachers, with their eyes to the past and the future, less figural.

So often in school, children are told that what they are learning will help them later in life, even if they aren't interested and can't understand why. Insufficient attention is paid to exploring what is relevant and necessary to the children's lives now. More attention should be paid to finding relevant applications that can be part of their learning. In our experience, any subject can be transformed to the immediate interests of students. The range goes from chocolate chip math, which permits students to eat their correct answers, to role-playing the characters in a story. In between, spelling words are taken from children's readings and from mistakes in the student's own writing. Vocabulary lists come from words related to the expressed enthusiasm for activities outside of class, and writing and reading are based on curiosity. There is a history of making science projects and social studies relevant, and the study of the arts can naturally be used to encourage spontaneous self-expression.

In addition to the learning that results from greater classroom involvement, teaching that taps students' immediate interests provides conditions for here and now interpersonal experiences that are the substance of building an interactive relationship. The draw between the students and the teacher is their common interest in what is happening in class at the time that it is happening. Sharing challenging work provides a set of appropriate educational experiences that form the basis for classroom relationships to grow.

A Gestalt view of how this growth takes place is insightful. Every living organism strives for comfort, but the feeling of comfort becomes more complex as organisms become more complex. For humans, deep emotional interconnections with other people are part of the dynamic. It is also possible to avoid interacting intimately with other people by finding enough comfort through satisfying only needs for food and shelter (however extravagant), the work that is necessary to provide them, and entertaining activity to fill time that is left over. When interpersonal history becomes too painful, there arises a strong need to defend oneself from the risks that are involved in relationships. Therefore, the search for comfort can move in either direction, for or against the deepening of relationships.

What explains this human complexity is the development of a personal concept of self—actually many selves that make up the whole. These various selves, including student selves, teacher selves, and the broad range of other roles that each of us plays, carry with them the history of their development, which defines what will count for comfort. Generally, the more pain that has been experienced, the more defended is the definition. Luckily, no self is absent of flux. The degree of flexibility and rigidity of the defenses varies within us and sometimes because of changes in the environment. In our view, human complexity, fortunately, also provides mechanisms that allow for lowering defenses—as it were, counterdefense mechanisms.

No doubt, each of our multiple selves must be defended in order to experience comfort. It is helpful, though, to think of defenses as the boundaries of the self. The idea of boundaries moves away from the concept of pure defensiveness to one that suggests more room for positive change. And from this vantage, it is not a far stretch to imagine boundaries that can be made more or less permeable. As they become more permeable, the opportunity for contact between two people increases, which we believe is the substance of a growing interactive relationship.

In Gestalt terms, contact is available to every human being and implies impact on both people. The experience necessarily changes each person. When people come into contact, the experience changes us because we are sufficiently open to take it in. Interactive relationships of this kind are imbued with the potential for high-level functioning. Though the energy for maintaining an openness to contact is itself not without bounds, openness is an optimal approach to teaching and learning.

There is a tendency to think that the intimacy of an interactive relationship only takes place between one person and another or, occasionally, among a small group of people. Figuring out how this type of relationship can be normal in the life of a typical classroom is the obstacle that has to be faced. It seems obvious there are too many people in a classroom to imagine that developing these relationships, all at once, is practical.

One answer lies in not assuming that relationships develop all at once. Over the course of a semester, there are occasions when a teacher and a student, one on one, have time to interact more deeply than usual. These moments are important to students, as they must be to teachers. They need not be limited, however, to interactions that only involve the two of them. Other opportunities occur in the regular flow of class activities. In our experience, we have found that listening intently to a student expound on his or her ideas or concerns, while keeping others from interrupting until it feels as though there has been enough time for the individual to be truly heard and understood, sometimes counts as importantly as a private conversation. Similarly, a few words of help, support, or understanding at a special moment can have a significant effect. Other opportunities exist when a teacher is giving feedback. All of this is part of building teacher-student relationships.

Outside of these interactions, the overall quality of the classroom's learning environment makes a difference. When interaction is encouraged among the students themselves, as well as with the teacher, an expectation for interactive relationships expands. With care to balancing the pressures of curriculum and process, a teacher can create a learning environment that is supportive, challenging, and highly enjoyable. The effect is contagious in the sense that caring for each other is valued and not difficult to practice by the teacher and the students. Responsibility for maintaining this learning environment is spontaneously shared by everyone. In spaces like this, where contact occurs, diversity becomes a valuable gift.

An awareness of fears makes them less figural, gives teachers more creative self-control, and supports an openness for contact.

Self-awareness prepares one for contact. Certainly, there are interactive relationships that develop without conscious processing, but it makes sense that teachers would want to be more proactive about achieving a contactful learning environment. Being proactive centers around noticing. Of course, noticing what is taking place in the context that surrounds one is critical. But noticing what is happening inside oneself is an even more important source of assuring contact.

What is there to notice? Everyday feelings are the obvious focus, in both the mind and the body. Thinking is an equally valuable source of data. Together, they are even more valuable. Less obvious are actions. What teachers do makes up the personal stories of "who am I" as a teacher; yet there are ways in which we act that are not clearly conscious. Bringing teacher stories to full consciousness is illustrated by the preceding chapter. Paying attention allows us to see the patterns of our actions and their effects on students.

What can happen when we notice? It is possible to identify the fears that raise defensiveness. Some of these fears are based on unsuccessful and unpleasant past experiences. Some are directly tapped by what is happening now. Either way, these fears need to be evaluated for whether they signal real or imagined dangers. It is usually unconscious fears that lead to dysfunctional behavior, in teaching as elsewhere in life. Fears are prone to puff themselves up in our fantasies about what ill might happen. Often, though, if credence is withdrawn from these fantasies, it is not difficult to find an adequate solution to what feels threatening. Even with imagined confidence, some control is available for shifting the figure in the ground.

Mindful choice leads more directly and functionally to one's goals. Yelling, for example, is a sign of panic and may be appropriate when one is startled. Habitually yelling, though, quickly becomes less and less effective. A fresh view of its stimuli and an effort to find alternative responses restore the lively interactiveness of a classroom. We can't expect to be conscious of all our fears, but recognizing their driving force, which steers us in unwanted directions, frees the ability to choose actions and reactions more creatively.

Student misbehavior can threaten a teacher's confidence and lead to unsuccessful coping. Bringing up one's defenses is a natural response to one's fear of failure, but it also has the effect of closing down the opportunity for contact. Students will react very differently when a teacher shows concern as well as displeasure. A clever choice is to reframe the confronting behavior in a direction that brings the student back to working with, not against, the class goals. A teacher's habitual behaviors that are not responsive to the specific situation are unlikely to succeed in making this happen. An aikido-like response that gracefully incorporates the misbehavior can sometimes make it an interesting addition to the lesson.

It is not only misbehavior that can threaten a teacher. Anytime there is a contradiction between what is happening in class and the goals that a teacher hopes to achieve, a teacher's confidence can be undermined. We assume that our efforts to facilitate students' learning will have positive effects on what they know and can do, yet so often we are wrong. Blaming students for failure, though understandable at times, also has the effect of closing out contact. If possible, it is more constructive to recognize our fear of failure and assume that, at bottom, teachers are responsible for finding ways to successfully help students learn, whatever their predisposition.

Teaching habits can get in our way. These habits are supported by assumptions that are often unnecessary and inaccurate—such as believing that when children are not quiet, they are not learning. By loosening what restricts us, by tapping our courage in the face of fears, it is possible to attenuate their hold on our behaviors. Above all, courage supports contact, and for teachers, the most effective signs are humor, empathy, and vulnerability. From this position students will feel the invitation for contact. Though the teacher has more power in relationships with students, there can be a balance in the expression of self.

Teacher behaviors that restrict contact—intellectualization, introjection, projection, splitting, and demanding confluence—signal unidentified fears operating in the classroom.

In contrast to empathy, humor, and vulnerability, which deepen relationship, there are patterns that teachers use that restrict contact, typically driven by unidentified fears. Fear is expressed in many ways, and this complicates matters. Fantasies about untoward consequences in the future—difficulties that trigger feelings of impending hurt—are the ones that blow up in our minds as potential catastrophes. Memories that tap past disappointments trigger feelings of wariness toward what seem to be similar situations in the present. In Gestalt terms, these memories are unfinished business waiting to be rectified. Until these fears are brought into awareness, they have the power to appear and reappear, creating negative emotional responses that are unwarranted in the present. The general effect is to make the present less figural and everyone more resistant to contact.

One familiar pattern of restricting contact is intellectualization. The ubiquitous shame and guilt that most students experience over the years, still gnawing in the teacher, are hidden behind a heightened importance of the intellect. The examples are various. A teacher affects an all-encompassing superior knowledge in order to aggrandize his or her power in the classroom. The teacher simply reasons intellectually that the threat of negative consequences will surely motivate how students act in class. And equally common is the belief that students will be motivated when they are told that what they have to do is for their own good. Rational answers to problems that confront us are assumed to be the only course of action, even though so often they don't solve the problems that exist.

Different than productive intellectual activity, intellectualization is when unwanted feelings are cut off and a teacher's unfinished business from his or her student years is unconsciously in the foreground. At the cost of a loss of emotional and body awareness, there is a momentary promise of control over students' behavior. The overall result is a loss of intuitive behavior because the intellect, feelings, and body awareness are no longer joined. In the classroom, when the teacher's intellect reigns, communication between the teacher and the students is necessarily diminished. Neither the teacher's nor the students' voices are fully heard.

Another typical pattern restricting contact is introjection: criticism, ideas, and advice from others are taken in too quickly. Our values begin with what we have been told by parents, other family members, teachers, or anyone else of past significance in our lives. At times, though, these people become disembodied voices in the mind that have not been carefully considered in terms of the growth and development of personal meaning. Commands are heard, coming from voices that are not truly our own, or maybe not even someone else's at this point, saying that this, and this, and this, and this is what we *should* do. When the values were originally expressed, as well as in the present, there was little consideration of whether these *shoulds* are actually valuable to us. Such criticisms, ideas, and advice need to be reevaluated.

For example, a teacher may have introjected the notion that students should do homework every night. When nothing really relevant exists to assign, however, the work is not meaningful and has to be rationalized. So we might hear a teacher say, "You must develop the habit of doing homework." Introjection interferes with interacting with students honestly, particularly in the here and now where contact happens. A more fruitful struggle is to examine the assumption of doing homework every night. It may be possible to recognize where the pattern came from and discover what fears get in the way of being more flexible.

Restricting contact runs deeper yet when there is a distortion of the emotional connection between a teacher and a student. This happens when a teacher projects his or her discomforts onto a student. Projection is likely when we find ourselves name-calling. A student is seen as lazy—or mean, disinterested, shy, angry, needy, and so on—not really because it is so but because the teacher feels this way about him- or herself. Even fears of math can lead to imagining similar fears in others; no less, a poor self-image as an artist might lead to a teacher telling students that they have no talent. Projection helps to calm a teacher's fears by locating the problems in the students, but it complicates his or her relationship with students by confusing the real problems they present with invented ones.

Splitting, like projection, is another pattern that reflects an emotional distortion. In this case, the interference with contact stems from seeing only extremes in ability and behavior. Students are judged good or bad—with little regard for the many subtleties that describe any human being so much more accurately. Without noticing the myriad of individual differences, a teacher can't find a sensitive fit between the needs of the child and classroom goals. The tendency to split is colorfully illustrated in an earlier chapter in the story about role-playing. When undergraduates studying to be teachers are asked to enact students who are difficult to work with, the only option they recognize is to misbehave outrageously—even those in the group who weren't asked to play this role joined in spontaneously. In spite of being forewarned that useful role-playing requires some subtlety, there seemed to be only two choices: good students and bad students. From this vantage, contact is improbable.

The height of restricting contact—sometimes involving the worst kind of emotional abuse—occurs when there is a demand for confluence. Hoping to establish firm control over students' feelings and behavior, teachers press students to think and feel as they do. It's difficult enough for a child to be labeled bad; how much more damaging it is when a teacher says to the class, "Don't you agree that Johnny (or Suzy) is a bad boy (or girl)?" Oddly, the control over classroom behavior is often ephemeral because students persistently seek opportunities to escape this emotional tyranny. However, the loss of self that results from a child giving up personal wants and needs may be long lasting.

Unlike other efforts at masking authentic emotions in an attempt to avoid awareness of painful feelings, the demand for confluence tends not to be limited to particular instances of classroom interaction. The problem is heightened to the extent that teachers demand the expression of identical feelings and want more and more for students to be their copies. The effect is often pervasive and is especially nonconducive to interpersonal contact.

There are other psychological patterns of restricting contact that occur in ordinary daily life, but luckily we don't find them frequently expressed in teacher-student relationships. Our work is not meant to deal with conditions that involve, for example, anger turned toward oneself, out-of-control rage, or serious depression. Yet all of these patterns of restricting contact, both the ones we do and the ones we don't address, have in common an aim to protect a person from emotional hurt, however harmful they are in the end. Our goal, in contrast, is for teachers to strive for awareness even though it may foster discomfort. In the short run, awareness may seem to make matters worse—including possible painful interactions. However, this is the only path a teacher can follow when clearly setting out to develop interactive relationships. The goal to build relationships in all arenas of life takes work, and the effort required in the classroom must be as authentic as that anywhere else.

Undermining assumptions, practicing direct language, listening without interrupting, and participating in variations of role-playing are means of experimenting with and increasing contact.

One might imagine that it is impossible to avoid teaching habits that discourage relationships with students without years of psychotherapy. We have found, though, that simple activities provide opportunities to try out new ways for interacting with students. These activities, which we have facilitated in the "Art and Science of Teaching" classes and staff development workshops, expand the possibilities that teachers can choose from when faced with everyday classroom problems. The underlying strategy is to experiment with acting differently in a safe learning environment. The teachers' common task is to notice what behaviors feel authentic and potentially useful. As facilitators, we challenge people to stretch themselves into places where fears hold them back—with the assurance that they will be appreciated for their efforts. No matter the result, the group discussions that follow are always insightful.

Undermining assumptions

One of the simplest activities—called "I see, I imagine"—provides an immediate sense of how unwarranted assumptions interfere with communication. Taking turns, a participant observes a partner and makes a comment that begins with "I see." This is followed by a second comment beginning with "I imagine." Some examples are "I see you have no makeup on. I imagine you are shy"; "I see you are wearing a hat in class. I imagine you have a rebellious streak"; or "I see your hair is messed up. I imagine you got up late and are still tired."

In a discussion, it's easy for people to recognize that the assumptions aren't necessarily true. It's also easy to understand how thinking someone is shy, rebellious, or tired, when this description is not congruent with his or her self-perception, can result in disconnected communication. Once the problematic effects of habitually jumping from observation to imagination are discussed, there is a tendency for teachers to continue questioning their assumptions about students.

Practicing direct language

A more difficult experiment requires learning about communication that invites contact. Direct language expresses feelings held by the speaker. People are likely to respond directly to directness. Indirect language speaks more about the listener's feelings, and it typically brings up defensiveness, especially with regard to negative messages. So instead of saying to a student, "You are rude," a teacher might say, "I am offended." The change in the choice of words doesn't promise magical changes in a classroom, but the psychological climate for developing a relationship is improved.

More complicated examples abound. It is not surprising to hear a teacher say, "How could you do that? What's wrong with you?" Such questions can hardly be met with anything but a defensive attitude, or sometimes harsh words, from the student. They are an unnecessary indictment and could be easily replaced by, "I am frustrated with how you are behaving!" or even in a more caring way,

"I can't figure out what you need now." Other examples of indirect language are "Do you think this is acceptable behavior in class?"; "Don't you care about any-one but yourself?"; or "Who do you imagine is going to clean up this mess?" Communication is improved when such questions are changed to statements that begin with "I resent," "I feel," or "I want."

It is common in our culture for displeasure and resentment to be couched in terms that blame the offending person rather than speaking about personal feel-ings such as hurt, anger, or disappointment. A contrasting cultural norm that makes it awkward to express positive feelings toward someone adds to the com-plexity of using direct language. We're not talking about ordinary compliments for work well done, nor is it a matter of liking (or disliking) a child. Rather, it is a matter of recognizing behaviors and traits that make for a student's unique personal achievements and/or contributions to the successful functioning of a classroom. Even in a high-functioning classroom, obstacles created by the use of indirect language hinder contactful, let alone respectful, interpersonal relation-ships.

It is profitable at times to bring these obstacles to the surface and model alter-natives. One can practice direct language. One group exercise directs partici-pants to use "I" statements when relating a classroom experience. This is a fruit-ful place to start. Another exercise asks participants after working together in a class or workshop to gather in a circle and express their appreciations and resent-ments to the other group members and the leader(s). They are instructed to begin each statement with the name of the person to whom they are speaking and to follow that with either "I appreciate . . ." or "I resent. . . ." This experi-ence, if care is taken to demand a match between the positive and the negative, brings to awareness difficulties with either or both of these expressions of feel-ings. The willingness of teachers to take responsibility for their feelings is essen-tial. By modeling this behavior, teachers can expect the students to do the same.

Listening without interrupting

Similar to the idea that teaching is telling, the notion of discussion is often asso-ciated with taking turns speaking. The idea that discussion is mainly about lis-tening is not predominant. An interactive classroom requires shifting the focus from speaking to listening or at least to balancing the two. With this change, there is a firmer ground for taking for granted that teachers should be good listen-ers. The skill is quickly rewarded with an improved climate for learning. Yet at-tempts to improve listening skills are rare. We find that it takes no more than setting up exercises whereby two people take turns listening to examples of each others' tutoring or teaching experiences without interruption to bring listening into consciousness. Whether a report focuses on problems or stories of success is not critical, but to improve listening, practicing not interrupting is.

Some of the things that get in the way of careful listening are the fear of not getting a turn, worrying and planning about what one wants to say, and asking questions that reflect the concerns of the listener more than those of the speaker. To the extent that what is told is highly determined by the listener's questions and comments, the speaker is less likely to feel that it is his or her story. An exchange becomes an exercise in listening when one person is expected to pay focused, nonjudgmental attention to another and each is responsible for retelling the partner's story as accurately as possible.

When the two people have finished hearing each other, they take turns sharing with another twosome what was heard without assistance from their partner. There is little guarantee in ordinary listening that a self-conscious awareness of the process takes place. These "restrictions" heighten sensitivity to the act of listening.

Role-playing student and teacher shoulds

Role-playing is the most familiar form of activity that encourages experimenting with self in relationship. In its simplest form, class or workshop mates exchange roles as a student and a teacher confronting each other with their "shoulds." The "teacher" expresses to the "student" a series of statements that begin with, "As a student, you should. . . ." Irrespective of personal feelings about the matter, the partner in the role of the student says, in every case, "Yes, I should." The second person then takes a turn at expressing her or his "shoulds" and receives the same positive answer. The exercise produces a wide range of responses that include everything anyone ever wanted from students. The result is a powerful release of each teacher's hopes and ideals and the students' sense of oppression. This is a helpful awareness, but we are looking for something more.

The tables are then turned. Now "students" tell the "teachers" what they should do. In the same fashion, each person starts with, "As a teacher, you should. . . ." However, the answer is not automatic. The "teacher" is instructed to decide between one of two responses: "Yes, I should" or "No, I should not." Later, there will be time for discussion and qualifications, but for the moment, the activity is meant to pressure the individual for a temporary choice— recognizing that in everyday life such choices are often necessary. The goal of the activity, with attention to both parts, is for the teacher self that is embodied in each of us to experience the tensions that exist between the wants of students and teachers. When wants are congruent, there are few issues to deal with, but when they conflict, there is much to think about and discuss. The conflicts lead to and energize the discussion.

A good example is when a "student" says to his or her partner, "As a teacher, you should always take each student's individual needs and abilities into account," and the "teacher" answers after a moment's hesitation, "No, I should not." In a typical discussion, the teacher will defend the answer by complaining that there are just too many students in a normal class to attend to each individually. Other group members are sure to bring up ways in which they think it is feasible. It is helpful when people mention that one doesn't have to respond to every student's needs at every moment, that there are times when a teacher can respond to many students' needs simultaneously, that some needs will be met outside of class time, and a variety of other creative possibilities. Inherent in these contributions to the discussion is the belief that a teacher should work toward meeting individual needs. Only with this belief will teachers be motivated to search for possibilities.

Role-playing for problem solving

More demanding forms of role-playing—in the sense that creative responses are required—are used to flesh out new and creative ways of acting as a teacher. Participants are given the role of either a teacher or a student and asked to rethink problems that have been raised in discussion. The problems can stem from ideas in the readings or, more often, from unsuccessful experiences in field work in local schools. The role-play provides an opportunity to replay what might take place with a set of new behaviors. In an effort to find what might work better, participants are encouraged to exaggerate their ideas and make paradoxical responses. Humor is an important element in role-playing. This climate supports the courage to reframe and unstick stuck places.

Exploring intrapersonal conflicts

"Warm seat work" is the most demanding form of role-play for teachers. We developed this technique as an adaptation of the hot seat/empty chair technique that Gestalt therapists integrate into a larger body of psychotherapeutic techniques. In counseling, all the roles are played by the client, who moves back and forth between two chairs as a means of clarifying who is speaking at the moment. The therapist acts as a coach who suggests what roles to play—assisting and encouraging as need be. In therapy, an integral goal is to go deeply into the emotional world. In warm seat work, we are careful only to pursue a replay of the characters and feelings that inhabit a teacher's life space.

The main goals of warm seat work are to understand one's own conflicting feelings, to empathize with the other people with whom one must interact, and to see more clearly what alternative behaviors are possible—particularly for oneself. One semester, Carol, an undergraduate, had been assigned to tutor in an elementary class of mostly Spanish-speaking children. She didn't know any Spanish and felt stymied about how she would relate to the students. Her fantasy, and fear, was the idea of having to function as a teacher with a child who speaks no English at all. Based on a conversation she actually had with the principal, Mr. Farnum, she agreed to move between the two chairs as she engaged in an imaginary conversation with him.

In the following warm seat dialogue, Carol articulates her paralyzing fear, faces it, and can then move on:

Carol: This is the first time that I've had experience going into a classroom, and I'm really apprehensive . . . not only being in the classroom for the first time but being that really most of the children are Spanish-speaking children. I don't have any background.

Jerry: Have Mr. Farnum answer you. What will he say to you now that you imagine?

"Mr. Farnum": I can appreciate your problem. I had similar feelings when I was assigned to the school, but it's working out, and I'll help you.

Jerry: Answer him back.

Carol: Great. (chuckle, group laughs)

Jerry: Tell him how you feel. Tell him how you feel really.

Carol: I feel as though if he could do it, maybe he could show me. (Jerry points to "Mr. Farnum.") Maybe you could show me your techniques, and I can catch on.

Jerry: (whisper) Tell him how you feel.

Carol: How do I feel? I feel nervous and apprehensive . . . and insecure. That's it.

Jerry: Do you feel worse than that?

Carol: No.

Jerry: You don't?

Carol: I think that's about as bad as you could feel as a teacher.

Jerry: Uh-huh. . . . (lots of hands go up in the class)

In the discussion that followed, several students gave Carol advice and encouragement. One student said she had the same field placement the year before, and she managed just fine. Another student said she had been in a similar school, and she offered specific hints like starting out by talking with someone who speaks English and Spanish equally well. Another said she was in a similar situation and was requesting to be transferred. Yet another said that her experience showed in classes like this that most kids spoke some English. The discussion closed with a perceptive question about assumptions: "On that first day you were there, did you imagine that they were only Spanish speaking, or did you just hear that the kids speak Spanish all the time?"

For Carol, the reality of the situation didn't match the strength of the insecure feelings. Once an awareness of them was reached, it was then possible for Carol to take in whatever advice was offered, mull over it, and believe in her ability to solve some of the problems that might arise.

Another time, a teacher portrayed two internal voices, one called freedom and the other, control. The source of the conflict was buried in the teacher's mind. An extensive conversation between the two voices revealed the virtues and limitations of both. Her classroom problems were buried in conflicting beliefs, and the discussion clarified the usefulness of learning to talk with one's selves. The clarity of inner conversation pointed to choices that had to be made: where she needed to take control and where she could offer freedom for making choices. Warm seat sessions, in general, stimulate new avenues for interacting that often lead to practical problem solving.

All of these activities for experimenting with one's teacher self in relationship with students derive their power from heightened self-reflection. The activities broaden the field of awareness, the ground, making it possible to notice detail and perspectives that have been missed. The results facilitate the ability we are born with to shift our focus of attention, thereby changing what is figural. Behavior is less likely to be habitual and potentially more experimental.

Both teacher learning and student learning prosper in the adventure of creating contactful relationships.

Teaching in our view is an ongoing experiment, particularly experimenting with teacher self in relationship with students. In Gestalt theory, the aim is to become aware of restrictive behaviors, consciously inhibit them, and encourage others in ways that open up opportunities for contact. However, the outcomes of how we interact with others are unknown, anywhere in life, so all of a teacher's life can only be viewed as exploration of possibilities. Fundamentally, there is no rehearsal for any particular act of teaching, and there is certainly none for the moment of learning. We must constantly encourage ourselves to make small, new, more functional and satisfying moves because it is simply a sensible way of life for a teacher. This is the meaning of the development of a teacher self, and there is no end to the process. We are always in a position to improve.

Vitality and liveliness in the classroom are sure signs of a teacher and students in a contactful relationship. They are indicative of a teacher who is in touch with an authentic and truer self. In this kind of classroom, there is an expression of strengths and a willingness to recognize weaknesses. The teacher is aware of the responsibility that a person in power should have. Such a teacher is able to invite students to express clear wants, needs, expectations, demands, appreciations, and resentments. This is an educational environment that has both ease and excitement, for it is one where all the players feel their voice and agency. The alternative is where teachers experience themselves burning out after even just a few years in the classroom. The frustrations and difficulties of being a teacher are better addressed by an environment in which interpersonal contact provides a sense of adventure.

Epilogue

The semester after choosing all of the student stories that would be woven into the larger story we've told, I read two paragraphs in Paul Dixon's final paper that captured the essence of developing a teacher self:

"Then, out of nowhere, during the question-and-answer segment of my group's panel discussion, it hit me, BAM!!! At this point, I can't remember the exact words that triggered it, but when I went home I finally figured out what I think this whole semester is about. We needed to read our books in order to realize that we didn't need to read our books. Huh? I know I may sound kind of nonsensical, but there is a lot of logic behind these thoughts. You see, what is really important is for us as teachers to find the teacher inside of us. We don't need someone else telling us how to solve our problems in the classroom; we need to do what feels natural. All of the men and women who wrote the books we have read this semester knew that and are simply telling us how they did it.

"My idea may sound a little far-fetched, even crazy, but what you must realize is that the idea is not mine. All of the authors that we have read must have known it or their books would be very similar. If we as teachers attempt to teach our students in a way someone else told us to, we are doing them more harm than good. We can only teach one way and that is our own way. In order to help my students I must teach them the best way I can, not the best way Kohl, Williams, Murdock, or Rogers can. This, in my opinion, is the single greatest lesson I learned this semester, and I hope the rest of my classmates did for their students' sake."

Paul startled the class with the announcement of his insight. In the discussion, students loudly defended the readings, the need to learn from the experiences of others, and even me—as if my honor were at stake. I was quiet. I agreed with Paul, and still I had no problem assigning the next week's reading at the end of class. Life is full of paradoxes, and like everyone else, Paul did the assignment.

Index

About the Author and Coauthors

ABOUT THE AUTHOR

Retired from the College of Education at Temple University, **Jerome S. Allender** still works with teachers to discover more about the teaching and learning process. His research continues with colleagues in the American Education Research Association's Special Interest Group: The Self-Study of Teacher Education Practices. He lives in Philadelphia with his wife, Donna, and divides his time among writing, family, travel, and playing classical and jazz trumpet.

ABOUT THE COAUTHORS

Crystal L. Hicks (now Hay) lives in the beautiful mountains of southwestern Pennsylvania where she is a full-time mom. That's plenty for her right now. **Tracy L. Burns** (now Stewart) is a full-time mom too, although she has a clear aim to be an educator in a zoo one day.

Joann Russo, who was in advertising, and **Shaari R. Mersack,** who was in retail sales, recently left their first jobs after graduating from college to become teachers—when they realized that, after all, teaching is in their hearts. **Bryant V. Chavous,** a ninth grade math teacher, simply says teaching gives purpose to his life.

Shawn Poole, Hollie Gilchrist, and **Jennifer Pakola** have focused their careers on teaching in Philadelphia city schools. Shawn, a kindergarten teacher, sees his larger work as a struggle for educational reform. Hollie balances teaching fifth and sixth grade children with graphic design. Jennifer adds to teaching first grade her work with other teachers in the Philadelphia Writing Project.

Tracy A. Heal (now Montague) is an elementary school teacher in western Montana. She shares her interest in hiking, fishing, and hunting by involving her students in community ecology projects. **Stephen E. Trois** combines everyday teaching with his love of writing—currently a book about the sinking of the Titanic. **Rachel Allender** recently resigned as the director of the photography program at Drexel University. She is now redefining her professional career through graduate studies in the field of social work.

Donna Sclarow Allender is currently a Gestalt therapist. By the time Donna retired from teaching, she had been in elementary school classrooms for over thirty years. In 1970, she cofounded the Project Learn School in Philadelphia—an open-classroom parent-cooperative school that lays its claim to fame because it still thrives.